MW01688099

Become a Student of Your Students

Other books by Daniel Bobinski:

Creating Passion-Driven Teams

Hire, Train, & Retain Great Employees

Removing Obstacles to Success

How to Train Other People

The Teacher's Intellect:
Creating Conditions for Teaching & Learning
(with Dennis R. Rader)

Become a Student of Your Students

Daniel and Jeralynne Bobinski

LEADERSHIP
DEVELOPMENT
PRESS

A Division of LEADERSHIP DEVELOPMENT, Inc.

Become a Student of Your Students
Daniel Bobinski
Jeralynne Bobinski

ISBN-10: 0975943421
ISBN-13: 978-0-9759434-2-7

Second Edition published June, 2016

Published by Leadership Development Press
A division of Leadership Development, Inc.
10140 W. Meadowlark St., Ste. B, Boise, ID 83704

208-375-7606

Printed in the United States of America

Cover photo by Yanc, Used with permission
Cover design by Leadership Development Press and Lady Bug Press
Edited by Rose Sulfridge

Some names and identifying details have been changed to protect the privacy of individuals. Descriptions in some examples are amalgamations of known individuals. The pronoun "he" is often used in this book as part of an effort to keep the writing clean and simple. This is in keeping with AP guidelines; no sexism is intended.

Dedicated to

Leighton, Luke, and Abigail

Three of the most

awesome students ever

Become a Student of Your Students

CONTENTS

Preface

Most parents—if not all—want their children to be successful. We want our children to "have it better than we did." Therefore, most of us strive to provide a better life for our kids than we had growing up. It's an admirable goal, for sure, but unfortunately, too many of us don't know how to make that happen, or even where to start.

Sure, there are some things we know *not* to do, such as certain ways our parents treated us that we vowed never to do to our own children. But, rest assured, it's pretty much a guarantee that we're doing things to our kids that they will tell future friends (and maybe a counselor or two), "You wouldn't believe the way my parents acted whenever 'x' happened."

That fact aside, we know that since you're reading this book, you're interested far beyond the average parent in trying to make the greatest possible positive impact on your child. You're different. Not because you care more, but because you're actively looking for ways to create a stronger foundation for your child.

Creating a stronger foundation for children to grow into all God wants to them to be is our primary motivation in writing this book. Because so many parents have never been taught how, we want to provide a framework of understanding for how kids learn and grow.

Jeralynne knew from early on that she wanted to homeschool her children, and at the time of this writing she's been doing that for eight years. Daniel became an avid supporter of homeschooling when, while serving as a youth leader in his church, he noticed that it was significantly easier to talk with and engage the homeschooled kids.

With Jeralynne's degree in psychology and Daniel's degrees being in education along with 25 years of teaching emotional intelligence in the business world, we had a natural inclination to become students of our students. But along the way, we realized that so many parents did not have our backgrounds and certifications, and they were searching for answers. This book is a way for us to provide answers to many of the questions we've been asked over the years.

As a start, know that some of each child's makeup is nature (wired by God) and some of it is nurture (influenced by their surroundings). Also know that although we'll be presenting frameworks that are scientifically researched and highly validated, our intent is to keep things real and relevant, as opposed to theoretical and academic.

Some assessments and topics in this book you may recognize, and some of them may be new to you. Know that we certainly don't expect people to become experts in the areas we cover in this text. Our intention is simply for you to get a clearer picture of the unique ways your children learn and grow, and use that information to train up your children in the way they should go to the best of your ability.

Finally, we want you to know that the concept of "personality" has many dimensions and many facets, and there's no way to cover all aspects of personality in one book. Therefore, we decided to present what we believe to be the most practical aspects. Our main purpose is to help parents teaching in a homeschooling environment, but the material will be equally valuable if your student is attending an institutional (government/public or private) school.

Much more information on the areas we cover can be found online through targeted searches. As the title suggests, become a student of your students! Keep digging and keep learning as much as you can about them. The benefits will be many, and we're convinced that as you apply what you learn, your relationships with your children will grow deeper and richer. Another benefit: Your children will blossom and grow in the direction they were designed to grow. And, as they do that, they will feel more alive – and you probably will, too!

Acknowledgments

The adventure of homeschooling is one of the most fulfilling journeys a parent can take, and we are grateful that we get to do it. We are inspired every day by the children whose lives we get to touch, be they in our own homeschool environment, our homeschooling neighbors, or the other students we meet as we go about our day. The world around us is full of wonder, and we are grateful that the students in our lives are awed by the things they learn.

In addition to the children we get to teach,
we would also like to thank the following people
who have helped us in different ways:

Robert Croker

Alexandria Ford

"Miss Ginny" Garrett

Alex Goodman

Bailey Oui

The Families of FX

And a special thanks to
Leighton, Luke, & Abigail,
who love to learn.

Chapter 1
Train Up a Child in the Way He Should Go

From day one, kids start learning. And all children — even identical twins — have unique life experiences that shape their distinctive personalities. With Daniel being a certified behavioral analyst and holding a master's degree in education, and with Jeralynne holding a degree in psychology, we are convinced some of what makes up our personality is set in place by God, while other aspects are more impacted by our surroundings. Maybe you've heard these differences described as "nature versus nurture." However they're labeled, the components of anyone's personality are many, and with the infinite number of possible life experiences, no two people are exactly alike. Therefore, it is neither reasonable nor fair to try to put people into easily categorized boxes.

That said, parents *can* learn the fundamental differences in "personality." This would include the different ways people perceive and process information, behavioral style, and the core motivators that drive behavior, to name a few. Then, armed with that information, parents can be better equipped to "train up a child in the way he should go."

Unfortunately, too many parents don't take the time to learn about these differences. Such parents often go into default mode, adopting a belief that sounds like, "I went through school and learned just fine, so that should work well for my kids, too. If it worked okay for me, it will work for them."

To that we say, "Maybe, maybe not." And with certain personality and learning styles, our response is, "Absolutely not!" The same sun that melts butter will harden clay. For instance, a math curriculum that Emily loves, Sophie may hate. If Sophie's math scores don't look all that good, it doesn't mean that Sophie is bad at math (although some teachers can erroneously believe that Sophie isn't good at math if she isn't doing well with someone's chosen curriculum). In all actuality, it may be that Sophie is GREAT at math, but Sophie is wired very differently from Emily. Perhaps Emily likes rote drills and worksheets while Sophie likes hands-on learning with lots of conceptual exploration. The truth about students and learning is this: What works well for one doesn't necessarily work well for the other.

Whether you homeschool or have your children in a public or private school, being aware of your children's unique style will help you train up a child in the way he (or she) should go. The "career" of parenting is one for which we receive little training. Therefore, it is up to us to take initiative to learn how to be a good parent. This means we, as parents, must also become students. Allow us to suggest a framework to explore.

1. **Behavioral styles**: Are our kids task-focused, or people-focused? Do they like high risk, or do they prefer more calculated decisions?

2. **Hemisphericity**: Is the student more left-brained, right-brained, or whole-brained?

3. **Natural Intelligence**: Does the child have a natural inclination to math, or music, or nature, or visual things? What about logic, or action, or spiritual things? Or, are they innately drawn to words, or understanding emotions?

We will explore each of these areas in this book, and more. Every person alive has tendencies and preferences in these areas, and the differences among each of us in these areas are what makes each person unique.

As parents, we must be genuinely interested in our children as unique individuals. Our little ones (who grow up way too fast) are individuals with their own interests, curiosity, and skills. As we have observed, way too many parents talk "at" their kids and strive to manage or control them, rather than engage them in *genuine* conversation in order to learn the uniqueness of each child.

So how does all of this relate to the scriptural admonition to, "Train up a child in the way he should go"? A good explanation of Proverbs 22:6 can be found in *The Soncino Books of the Bible*, a set of Hebrew Bible commentaries edited by Dr. Abraham Cohen. Regarding Proverbs 22:6, Cohen says that the verb "train up" is derived from the Hebrew word for "education." He also tells us that the phrase "in the way he should go" is more accurately translated "according to his way." With those clarifications, we could paraphrase this verse to say "educate a child according to his way." Therefore, since the way Emily learns is not the way that Sophie learns, we should make adjustments in how we educate each of them!

Cohen also writes that the intention of Proverbs 22:6, "is not 'the way of uprightness and good living,' but 'for the way in which he is to spend his life.'" Cohen goes on to say the verse has to do with the type of occupations our children will have, and that our purpose as parents is to help them develop solid habits that will influence their conduct when they get out on their own.

You might ask, "What about teaching our kids to live uprightly and follow the Truth of the Gospel?" By all means, we should! In Deuteronomy 6:5-7 we are given the commandment to love God with all our heart, soul, and strength, and that this commandment is to be on our hearts. Verse 7 says of these commands, "Impress them on your children. Talk about them when you sit at home and when you walk along the road, when you lie down and when you get up."

But Proverbs 22:6 is touching on a different matter from Deuteronomy 6. Some parents innately "get" Proverbs 22:6, and others, not so much. So, let's look at this disparity -- and its ripple effects -- from the views of two sets of parents. One set of parents (let's call them Michael and Jessica) want their kids' career paths to follow their own. Michael works in construction, so he regularly points his kids to the trades. Since Jessica works as a bank teller, she suggests bookkeeping and other financial-oriented careers.

Because they have not paid attention to their children's attributes, when their son says he wants to be a speech pathologist and their daughter says she wants to go into horticulture, both Michael and Jessica downplay those ideas – and even scoff at them.

What Michael and Jessica failed to notice was that their kids had natural talents to succeed in those fields. With a little guidance, these parents could have selected classes and extracurricular activities for their children to help them thrive and become successful and fulfilled in their desired professions. Instead, their children became young adults who believed their own interests were invalid and that they'd have to go through life doing work they didn't really like.

On the other hand, let's consider James and Lisa, who talked openly with their kids about their interests and attitudes on various subjects. James and Lisa noticed when their kids got excited about new things. They also paid attention to how their kids learned, including their decision-making processes and motivations.

As a consequence, when James and Lisa's kids talked about career options, conversations and decisions flowed easily. From that, their children were encouraged to take classes that interested them, and they had a confident expectation that they would be successful in their future careers. And it was true. As adults, James and Lisa's children found their chosen careers to be fulfilling, and the ripple-effect was a confidence that spilled over into other aspects of their lives.

Now for the proverbial question: "Which type of parent would you rather be?" Assuming you want to be like James and Lisa, then you've chosen to raise up your child in the way he should go. And, as you go through this book, you will learn powerful ways to help make that happen. However, to be successful in this effort, you must agree to a fundamental understanding: What worked well for you in your education might not work for your kids. However, the only way to learn what will work is to become a student of your students.

The bottom line is this: If we want our children to become who God created them to be, we must seek to follow the Biblical instruction to educate each child according to his way.

Chapter 2
Intentional Parenting

We know a parent who couldn't wait to have children mainly because she wanted cute kids to dress up and show off. Said more bluntly, the mother really just wanted live versions of the dolls she had as a kid. Unfortunately, when her children got older and no longer want to be "mommy's fashion dolls," that parent felt rejected.

We know other parents who were ambivalent about having children, but once they had kids, they found they liked having their ego stroked. As parents, they became automatic authority figures, and it was a role they loved to play. Focus on the kids? Only as much as was needed to feel a sense of authority.

Still other parents have children to fill some aspect of their lives that are missing. We know a father who was active in sports in his youth, and he wanted kids so they, too, would be active in sports. By living vicariously through his children, the man was seeking to restore the youth he consciously (or subconsciously) sensed was fading away. We've also seen women who want daughters so they will do all the same things they did in their youth.

And we've know some people who had children because they believed it was a guaranteed way to always have someone love them. Consider the woman who never felt loved or appreciated by her own parents. She eagerly wanted children, believing that because those children would be dependent on her, she would always have people in her life that would love her. The problem? She was too clingy, and when her children pushed away she felt rejected.

The situations we're describing here fall more along the lines of co-dependency than love. Co-dependency often results in poor boundaries and little or no true discipline. Unfortunately, it also tends to create monster-like children who do not respect their parents – nor anyone else.

Our suggestion: Instead of parenting with any of the above methods, choose intentional parenting.

Parents Who Didn't Want to be Parents

Another part of the parenting spectrum are those who became parents against their will. We clearly remember meeting a set of parents who became parents "by surprise." They viewed their child as an anchor that interfered with their lives and slowed them down. Sadly, they openly talked about this in front of their child, who was old enough to understand what they were saying!

Then there was the parent who believed all children – even his own – were mean, evil, and selfish. He begrudgingly spent time with them, but mainly as a way to get his wife "off his back" (his words).

Still another parent we know thought she wanted children, but when she finally had one, she thought they were too much work. She complained daily about all the sacrifices she was making, and when she got tired of tending to her toddler's needs, she would walk out of the room, saying to her husband, "You watch her -- I'm done with her for the day."

Of course, there's also the parent who acquiesces to having children because his/her spouse wants them. Children in these situations are not really wanted by the one parent, merely tolerated. Often the parent who wanted children in the first place over-compensates with boundary-less "love." Again, not good.

Grace, Mercy, and Golden Nuggets

Hopefully you don't fall into any of the categories listed above, but if you do, grace and mercy are available in abundance from the Lord. And we offer you our grace and mercy, too. Perhaps you had poor relationships with your parents or had unrealistic ideas about parenthood. Perhaps your own upbringing had deep pain or tragedy that affected your attitudes about having children. The truth is, most people are unequipped to become parents, so if nobody taught you or modeled how to be a good parent, how could you possibly know?

Following the example of our Lord, we graciously open our hearts and say, "Today is a new day and you have the ability to choose differently!" We suggest "intentional parenting." Here's what it means:

Intentional:	done on purpose; deliberate
Parenting:	raising, bringing up, looking after, and taking care of children

We strongly believe the content of this book provides valuable ideas for you to improve your relationships with your kids, as well as set them on a path to greater fulfillment in their own lives. It's about raising up your children (in the way they should go), and it's done on purpose. That requires a deliberate choice from you. We call it intentional parenting.

By the way, if you were fortunate to have learned good parenting skills and you have already been doing a great job raising your kids, hats off to you for striving to be an even better parent. This book may cover some things you already know, but we trust that you'll still find a few "golden nuggets" of information to help you on your parenting journey.

Why Intentional Parenting is Beneficial

Here's a great reason to practice intentional parenting:

You'll get to know your children better,
and you might find that you actually like them.

We make that statement because most parents love their kids, but that doesn't mean they actually *like* them as people. Think about it. How many times have you heard parents saying they crave adult conversation after being around their kids all day? When we hear that, we often wonder if the parent is even *trying* to have decent conversations with their kids. Too often we see parents placating their children with nods, or even worse, baby talk.

Getting to know your kids as individuals is pretty cool. If you've never tried it before, you might be surprised that they're capable of more intelligent reasoning than you give them credit for. You might also be surprised to learn that they have a great sense of humor, that they really are interesting, and that they have uncanny insights about things. You might even find yourself glowing inside when you get a glimpse of how they're going to be as adults.

Consider the example of Michael and Jessica from the previous chapter. They talked *at* their kids, not *with* them, and look at the results. On the other hand, James and Lisa engaged their children as growing human beings. They invested their time and attention to learn the thoughts and emotions of their children. They were slow to anger, and overflowing with patience, and look at how those results were different.

Beyond the benefits to the children, another personal benefit of becoming a student of your students is that you will have a stronger relationship with them. Perhaps you've seen kids hit their teen years and suddenly become monosyllabic in their conversations with adults.

> How are you doing?
> *Fine.*
> Anything wrong?
> *Nope.*
> What's going on?
> *Nothing.*

Wouldn't you rather have this?

> How are you doing?
> *Pretty well. I'm a little concerned about Francis, but other than that, I'm doing okay.*
> Anything wrong?
> *He's been acting funny lately. Kind of distant. I don't know for sure.*
> What's going on?
> *Well, I think I may have offended him with a joke I told. I think he took it personally, but that's not how I intended it at all. I'm wondering if I should go apologize to him. At least then I'll know if it's me that has been causing him to be reserved lately.*

Which type of conversation would you rather have with your teen? The second conversation is the result of trust that develops as we focus on our kids and are there for them, mentally and emotionally, over a long period of time. There's been a solid history of listening, and not a lot of lectures.

When you see the first type of conversation (with monosyllabic responses), it is often a symptom that the child does not feel safe to express his or her views. Perhaps it's been too many lectures, or a history of the child not feeling heard, or maybe even feeling criticized too often. Often it's a combination of multiple factors. In any case, according to Daniel Amen, M.D., children who don't grow up in a safe environment will continue to be looking for ways to be safe in adulthood. Therefore, if we want our children to stand tall and be confident as adults, it's important for us as parents to create an environment in which our children feel safe and understood when they're with us.

In our opinion, lecturing is a technique that is one of the most difficult to remove from our parenting repertoire. Why is lecturing so hard to drop? Because it's so efficient! It's quick. It allows us to impart our wisdom in a matter of minutes. Unfortunately, even the most well-intended one-way words of wisdom will often have the opposite effect of what we wanted. Lectures are often a tool for building walls between us and our kids.

The late best-selling author Stephen Covey often talked about the difference between effectiveness (doing the right things) and efficiency (doing things quickly; that is, without wasting time). Covey said we make a mistake when we try to be *efficient* with people. According to Covey, when dealing with people, "Slow is fast and fast is slow." In making his point about this, Covey once remarked, "Try being efficient with your teenage daughter."

Essentially, we can only be efficient with things. We must strive to be *effective* with people, and that takes time. And allow us to suggest a crazy notion, but your children want to be understood! Being heard is one thing, truly understanding someone is quite different. It takes energy and effort. And yes, you may understand your children, but do your children feel understood? There's a big difference between the two.

Janet is a mother of several children who are now in their late teens and early 20's. When her children were young and just entering school, Janet attended several of Daniel's management workshops. In the section on listening skills, one assignment was to, "Try the listening techniques with anyone, and see how they work." Janet decided to try her newly learned skills with her small children, and she was amazed at the results. At the next workshop she couldn't wait to share what happened.

> I picked my kids up from school, and as usual, began asking how their day went. But this time, instead of just nodding my head, as they started telling me, I started to listen – *really* listen. In their voice tone I heard their emotions. In their words I felt their excitement. And, when I responded to their story in a way that acknowledged their feelings, their eyes got big and they looked surprised. I could tell they truly felt heard – and their faces showed that they thought it was great! What a difference it makes to truly listen to your own children!

When your children truly feel heard, they will *know* you care about them. And, with that knowledge in their hearts, they will trust you more, and they'll converse with you more, and you'll get to know them more.

That said, don't think all this comes naturally! We, too, had to learn how to do these things. And, as we'll see in the next chapter, becoming a student of your students does not come by osmosis. We must study and learn, and we must *want* to study and learn. So you know, here are the ripple effects of applying what you'll learn:

> You'll listen to your children differently.
> You'll establish a stronger relationship with them.
> You'll learn what makes them tick.
> You might find that you actually like them, not just love them.

From an educational standpoint, if you know your children better, you'll save yourself a whole lot of guessing. From that you'll be able to make better decisions about how to train them up in the way they should go.

Chapter 3
Your Role in Training Up a Child

Within the family unit, parents are the leaders. It is with great sadness we see some parents actually relinquishing aspects of their leadership to their children in the hopes that that their children might like them more. Children should not run the house, and when parents allow children too much latitude, thinking, "Let them be kids, I'll rein them in later to teach them about rules and responsibility," they're setting themselves up for much angst when the child gets older. We've seen it time and again.

The phrase Jeralynne uses for preparing young children for life is the "reverse funnel effect." In this analogy, we say that when parents are letting kids run wild with little to no constraints, they are filling up the wide end of the funnel. During the child's formative years their boundaries are all over the place, with the parent thinking, "When they get older, I'll rein them in." Unfortunately, those expanded boundaries will resist being compressed as the parent tries to bring the child into the narrow end of the funnel, where more discipline, respect, and tighter boundaries will be taught. That compression brings friction, emotional distance, and, too often, rebellion.

In the reverse funnel effect, parents keep a much tighter rein on kids in their early years, being consistent and firm with boundaries and rules. Then, as the children get older, with boundaries and rules already in place, children can be given much more freedom and be trusted with greater responsibilities. The result is more joy for the children as they experience greater freedoms, plus they will be firmly established with solid self-esteem, knowing they're making wise choices.

Some parents think a tight enforcement of rules in a child's early years will cause children to think the parents are mean. They've got it backwards. What's mean is letting small children do whatever they want in their early years, essentially training them that life has no boundaries or rules, then clamping down when the child gets older, crushing their established perception that life is only freedom with no rules. It's that compressing and crushing that eventually leads to monosyllabic conversations and possibly even rebellion.

One technique that we've found works very well for maintaining rules and boundaries with an atmosphere of love and respect is called, "Jekyll-Hyde." In chapter 21 we'll talk about making learning safe, but growing up should be safe, too. Parents who get upset at things and then *stay* upset are letting their emotions damage their relationships. Using the *Jekyll-Hyde* method, when a parent sees a rule violation, the parent's response is quick and firm. Errors are pointed out firmly and sternly, correct behavior or attitudes are explained, and the matter is dropped, with the parent returning to being a pleasant, affectionate parent.

Some might question the need for a firm and stern response, suggesting instead that a softer conversation explaining the rules is easier on the child's psyche. Our response is that a soft, loving conversation when rules are broken gives the child exactly what he wants – a loving tone from his parents. So, if that's the way to get a soft, loving conversation, then, hey, "Let me break more rules!"

Children do not like firm and stern, so if that's what they get every time they break the rules, they won't want to break the rules. The key to success in using *Jekyll-Hyde* is to *immediately* switch back to being pleasant and affectionate after any disciplinary action.

By the way, in keeping with the principles (and benefits) of the reverse funnel effect, you'll find that as your children get older, you won't have to be anywhere near as firm or stern with them when they make a mistake. You'll reach a point where all you have to do is give them "that look." They'll know they crossed a boundary, and they won't want to do it again. The "look" need last for only a moment, and you won't have to lecture. You can just watch their faces and see the wheels in their heads spinning while they're learning from their own mistakes. It's actually a joy to see them growing up and becoming responsible, and it feels good knowing that you've taught your children to think for themselves.

Other Responsibilities of the Leader

In recent decades, the majority of material written for training leaders in the business world revolves around the phrase, "Know thyself." In other words, the better you know your own strengths and weaknesses, the better you can know how to be effective in your leadership role.

So what does it mean to *know thyself* in terms of being a leader? In Daniel's work with managers and executives over the past several decades, here's how he has presented it:

> Know your behavioral style. Know how you tend to behave in various situations so you are better able to manage your actions, and thus lead better. Know how you perceive and process information, how others might do it differently, and be collaborative in finding ways to get the best results. Know your own motivations, and what might be motivating others, too. Again, you'll be better able to manage your actions when working with others to achieve that desirous win/win, and thus lead better.

Much research has shown that self-awareness is a key component to emotional intelligence, and that emotional intelligence is the main differentiator between average leaders and top leaders in the business world. We would venture to say that it is also a key component differentiating average parents from highly effective parents.

Here's a definition of emotional intelligence that we like:

> A kind of intelligence or skill that involves the ability to perceive and assess one's own and other people's emotions, desires, and tendencies, and then choose the best course of action based on that perception to obtain the best result.

We believe the term *know thyself* is simply a shorter way to say, "Perceive one's own emotions, desires, and tendencies." Then, to be an effective leader in the home, we must also work to perceive the emotions, desires, and tendencies of our children. Review the attributes of, "Know thyself" at the top of the facing page from the perspective of a parent. With that, you can choose the best course of action to train up your children in the way they should go.

Therefore, as you read this book:

1. Identify your own tendencies and preferences
2. Identify the tendencies and preferences of your spouse
3. Identify the tendencies and preferences of your children

As we pointed out in the first chapter, becoming a student of your students so you can train them up in the way they should go means helping them find and follow the way *they* should go. It will take effort on your part, but that's part of being a leader in the home, and nobody ever said being a leader was easy. The "career" of parenting has a set of skills that must be acquired if you want to be successful, just like any other career.

Our purpose in this chapter has been to help parents understand their roles as leaders, not to teach good communication skills (which are necessary for training up children in the way they should go). If you think you would like to improve your communication skills with your children (and anyone else, for that matter), let us recommend the book, *Crucial Conversations*, by Kerry Patterson, Joseph Grenny, Ron McMillan, and Al Switzler.

Likewise, if you think you'd like to learn more about emotional intelligence (commonly called *EQ*), we would recommend Daniel Goleman's book, *Emotional Intelligence*. Just know that Goleman's book will give you a solid understanding of the subject, not teach you how to improve your EQ. If you wish to work on improving your EQ, you might consider picking up a copy of *Emotional Intelligence 2.0*, by Travis Bradberry and Jean Greaves. But we also believe that as you go through this book, you will gain much insight into the foundations of what these other books are discussing.

Chapter 4
Choosing to Value the Differences

We firmly believe that a parent's ability to *understand* and *communicate with* his or her children is key to each child's educational success. And, we also agree with a quote attributed to Albert Einstein:

Education is not the learning of facts,
but the training of the mind to think.

It's our observation that Einstein's definition of education is marginalized in many of today's so-called learning environments. Too often, kids are being told what to believe about something, or made to memorize facts without analyzing those facts for patterns or relevance. In other words, much of what passes for education these days is telling kids *what* to think, not *how* to think. Yes, children must know facts, but knowing what to do with those facts in the process of thinking is infinitely more important. Consider this statement:

Everyone has thoughts, but thinking is a learned skill. *

In order to teach our kids how to think, we first must understand how they perceive and process information. In other words, *how they learn*. And, because behavioral styles correlate directly to learning styles, the next five chapters of this book present a practical overview on how to identify the four core behavioral styles/learning styles, and ways we can adapt to styles different from our own.

To review these styles, we'll focus on the DISC Model, which is used extensively throughout the world and is based on observable human behavior. By the way, you might be surprised to know that classifying different types of behavior goes back beyond the time of Christ at least to the time of Hippocrates, in 400 B.C. After much observation of people, Hippocrates proposed that four main types of people existed. He believed each of the four temperaments were associated with bodily fluids, so he named the temperaments Sanguine, Melancholic, Choleric, and Phlegmatic.

In the 1920's, Carl Jung outlined four types of personality in a psychological sense, but it was William Marston, a psychology professor at Columbia University, who, in 1928, created what we now refer to as the DISC Model of behavioral temperaments. It was from his model that the DISC behavioral assessments we use today were developed.

Over the years, people have come up with different ways to present the concept of four different styles, and chances are you've heard about them in one way or another. But the fact remains: Four core styles exist, and you should know about them. If you've learned about the four styles using one set of terms, here is how they correlate:

William Marston	**Dominant** (Core D)	**Influencing** (Core I)	**Steady** (Core S)	**Compliant** (Core C)
McCarthy's Learning Styles	Type 3	Type 4	Type 1	Type 2
Hippocrates	Choleric	Sanguine	Phlegmatic	Melancholic
Gary Smalley	Lion	Otter	Golden Retriever	Beaver
Colors	Red	Yellow	Green	Blue
Social Styles	Driver	Expressive	Amiable	Analytical
Communication Styles	Directive	Emotive	Supportive	Reflective

Regardless of what terms you prefer, remember how to get the most from understanding them:

4. Identify your own tendencies and preferences
5. Identify the tendencies and preferences of your spouse
6. Identify the tendencies and preferences of your children

The idea in becoming a student of your students is NOT to change them, but to learn their preferences so you can value them as the people God made them to be. Because behavioral styles are wired from birth, that is, "God given," it's important to remember we aren't supposed to try to rewire people. Obviously, each style has its pros and cons, and also some rough edges, and we'll address those some of those. But if you start criticizing someone's style or try changing who God designed them to be, it's going to end badly.

Remember that the phrase, "Train up a child in the way he should go," can also be translated, "Educate a child according to his way." If you think about training grape vines, the idea is to get the vines accustomed to growing a certain way. With grape vines, if you wait too long without any training, the vines harden, and they cannot be altered or the vines will crack and break.

With that in mind, know that each of the four DISC styles prefers to grow its own unique way. We don't want to force them into a direction they weren't designed to grow. If we criticize a child's style or try to force an unnatural change (i.e., try to force someone with a core "I" style to become more like someone with a core "C" style), those trainings will inhibit full development of who that person was meant to be. Then, as the child gets older, those "trainings" start to harden, just like a grape vine does. Later, when the child tries to revert to who God designed him to be, it's difficult. In fact, like the vines, the inside of the person can "crack and break."

By the way, another reason it's vital that we *train up the child in the way he should go* is that regardless of what kind of vine they are, their branches have to be off the ground or the fruit they're going to produce will be rotten and spoiled! Translated: The fruit of their lives won't be very good.

In all of this, a phrase you can keep repeating to yourself is, "Value the Differences." We say *value the differences* because, in reality, you have a choice: You can criticize someone's style, or you can choose to value it. Remember that each style has strengths AND weaknesses (what we call sometimes call *blindspots*). If you criticize someone's natural style, it's like saying they're wrong. Who wants to hear that? Of course, if you want to destroy your child's self-esteem, go ahead and criticize who God created them to be. But if your goal is to help your child, you need to value his or her strengths, even if those strengths are vastly different from yours.

Focus on Your Child's Strengths

Ask anyone who has found their life's passion, and they'll tell you that they play to their strengths. Try to get someone to improve an area of weakness, and they'll probably describe it as banging their head against the wall. Therefore, do not waste energy trying to get your children to lose or overcome their blindspots. The return on investment is just not worth it:

> Let's say a person has a strength, and on a 1 – 100 scale, that strength scores an 80. And let's say that same person has a weakness that is rated at a 20. One might think that getting someone to improve their weak attribute with a 20 score by five points (to a 25) might mean the person's strength score would drop a mere five points (in this case to a 75).
>
> Interestingly, studies have revealed that for a person to improve a weakness score by a mere five points requires phenomenal attention and energy. So much so that a mere five percent gain in an area of weakness results in a 20-to-40 percent drop in a person's natural strength!

Obviously, we need to help our children find strategies to be more effective in their areas of weakness (some of which we'll cover in this book), but again, in no way should we try to change who they are. It doesn't matter if someone is a Michael Jordan, a Jim Carey, a Mr. Rogers, or an Albert Einstein, every style has strengths and every style has weaknesses. Coming to terms with your own strengths and weaknesses is part of *knowing thyself* – a key to being effective in life. As parents, we need to become aware of our children's strengths and weaknesses so we can educate them according to their way. Not only will we be able to help them learn better, but we can also help them know themselves, so they can be effective in life, too.

A couple of notes before we proceed with the next chapter:

1: DISC is a Neutral Language!

The concept of *right* and *wrong* cannot be applied to behavioral style. Behaviors can be effective and appropriate for certain situations, and ineffective or inappropriate in others. But to say someone's behavioral style is "right" or "wrong" should not be part of anyone's thinking.

2: The coverage of DISC in this book is restricted to providing an overview of the four "pure" styles.

In reality, thousands of DISC blends exist, and that's part of what makes each child unique. However, most of us have a "core" behavioral style, meaning one of the four styles will be predominate. On occasion, some people have equal strengths in two of the four styles, and *very* rarely, a person may have equal strengths in three styles. In our coverage of DISC, we're focusing on the characteristics of the four core (pure) styles. Your student may be quite strong in two of the styles, and maybe even three (Common blends include D/I, D/C, I/S, and S/C). If you find that you're having a difficult time identifying your child's core style, start by eliminating the style that your child is *not*. If your child is age 8 or older, you might consider having him complete a DISC assessment, available through Family Experience Ministries (familyexperience.net).

3: People adapt.

Just because someone tends to behave a certain way most of the time, it's never a guarantee that the person will behave that way all the time. People tend to adapt their behavior as they deem necessary, situation-by-situation. For example, most people behave a certain way while sitting in the stands watching their favorite sport team, and then behave very differently while attending a black-tie event with their state's governor. For this reason, we caution all students of the DISC Language to not put people in a box! People have tendencies in their behaviors, but those behaviors can switch on a dime if the person believes his/her normal preferences will be inappropriate for a situation.

4: DISC assessments mainly measure behavior, but they also correlate directly to learning styles.

We've mentioned that the concept of personality is HUGE. With that, no one assessment can fully encapsulate the many facets of anyone's personality. Therefore, know that in the following few chapters on DISC, we're talking about behavior and learning styles. DISC does not measure anyone's intelligence, values, skills, experience, or education levels. What DISC assessments do measure is behavioral style (a person's preferred manner of doing things), all of which is observable. Thankfully, for those of us trying to help our students learn, DISC correlates to learning styles.

**"Everyone has thoughts, but thinking is a learned skill."*

This quote is original with Daniel and it is something he's been teaching his clients for years.

Chapter 5
The DISC Model and Learning Styles

As an overview, the four styles that Marston classified as Dominance, Influencing, Steadiness, and Compliance (resulting in the acronym DISC) correlate to learning styles (as established by Bernice McCarthy) in the following ways:

D = Type 3 learners
I = Type 4 learners
S = Type 1 learners
C = Type 2 learners

Why do behavior styles and learning styles correlate? Interestingly, just as Marston set up the DISC Model using two spectrums of preferences, educational experts used the same spectrums in differentiating learning styles. In learning styles, the first spectrum is about how people PERCEIVE information. The second is about how people PROCESS information. And, so that we're all on the same page, here are the definitions we're using for *perceiving* and *processing*:

Perceiving is becoming aware of something

Processing is performing a series of operations on something in order to preserve it

Perceiving

In learning, *perceiving* is how we first become aware of new information. At one end of the perceiving spectrum are people who like perceiving new information more conceptually, preferring to find meaning though objective, internal thinking. They often enjoy being introduced to new information through a task or simple activity that does not involve other people, and they enjoy a well-organized presentation from an expert source.

At the other end of the spectrum are people who prefer taking in new information experientially, usually with other people involved. They rely on their intuition and feelings, and want their learning to be more experiential and personal. They like being introduced to new information with an interactive activity, or at least by hearing and sharing stories that relate to the subject matter.

Think of it as a spectrum looking like this:

Conceptualizing
(thinking alone, with a task)

Experiencing
(feeling, with people)

Keep in mind that this is not an "either/or" proposition. Think of the light spectrum. In the light spectrum (e.g., the rainbow), light goes from red to orange to yellow to green to blue to purple. However, there is no place where one color suddenly stops and another starts; the colors simply blend along the way. Perception preferences are much the same way. A person's preference is almost always a blend of objective thinking and experiential feeling. Usually a person prefers one side or the other, but they can adapt as the situation warrants.

Two students we know, Ian and Sonya, like to perceive new data by some form of personal interaction with the material. As much as possible, Ian wants to interact with it in some way, while Sonya likes talking about it and what it means to her life.

On the other hand, Carl and Donna prefer to perceive new information through listening, and perhaps some kind of simple, practical task. As they listen to or watch new information be presented, they rarely talk, but you can see the gears moving inside their heads. Carl often remains very quiet, while Donna will eventually mention how she sees the new information can be used.

Processing

Now let's look at the Processing spectrum, which we'll draw as a horizontal line. We like to think of *processing* information as finding a place to file it in one's mental filing system. At one end of the spectrum are those who prefer processing new information through *active experimentation.* They are more comfortable with risk (believing they can go back and fix something if necessary), and they're more comfortable with making on-the-fly, quicker decisions.

At the other end of the processing spectrum are people who like to process by *reflection* and *observation.* They prefer taking their time when making decisions and are more comfortable with decisions that are low-risk. It's not that they can't make faster, higher-risk decisions, it's just that they prefer not to.

Reflective Observation ——————————— Active Experimentation

You may recall that both Ian and Sonya like to *perceive* information through personal interaction with the material, but once that information is perceived, they prefer to *process* it very differently.

The same is true for Carl and Donna. Both prefer taking in new information through listening, conceptualizing, or by working through some low-key, objective task. But they diverge in how they process new information.

As it turns out, both Donna and Ian like processing (that is, mentally filing) new data with active experimentation. They like to try out what they've just learned to see firsthand how it works.

On the other side of the spectrum are Sonya and Carl, preferring to review the material in a reflective manner, watching others, and contemplating internally how it might be applied to real life.

Four Distinct Learning Styles

When the Perceiving and Processing spectrums are overlapped perpendicular to each other, they create four quadrants. These four quadrants make up the four DISC behavioral styles – which just so happen to correlate to learning styles!

Below you can see how the two spectrums overlay to create the four behavioral styles and their associated learning style.

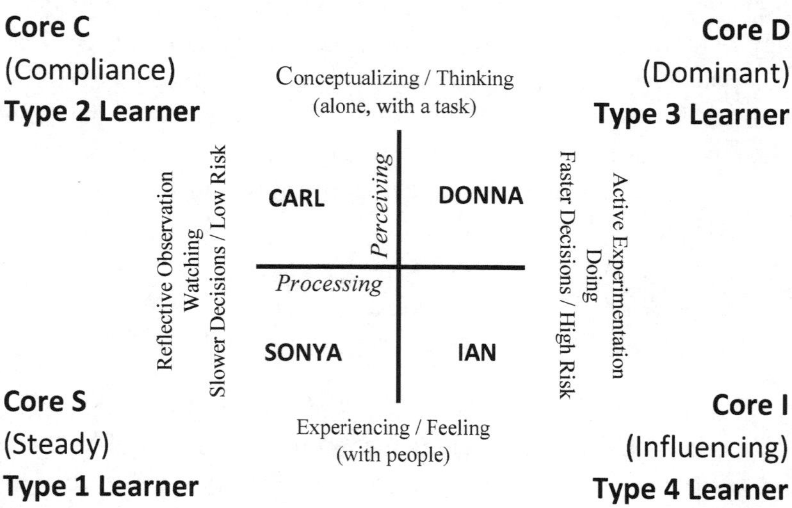

A Summary of Styles

Donna – Core D / Type 3 Learner

Donna's main interests are, "How does this work?" and, "How can I use this?" She values practical examples and practical application. Hers is a need for action – she wants to do something with what she's learning. Although she starts out mainly watching and listening, she processes best by hands-on activities that focus on real-world issues. Donna works well with deadlines and wants to know the results expected of her. She will then use that information to guide her decisions in how she completes her work.

Ian – Core I / Type 4 Learner

Ian's main interests are, "What if I adapted this to a different use?" and, "What if I tried this a new way?" He values big picture thinking and looks for ways to connect his new learning to other possibilities. His is a need for "what if" possibilities – he likes looking for ways to adapt what he's learning to achieve new solutions and new creations. Ian likes engaging new material by experiencing it, and he processes that new information the same way. He likes flexibility in his learning environment with open-ended assignments that for more creativity than trying to achieve pre-determined results. A shared vision of the future possibilities with a bit of fun, strategic competition inspires him to complete his work.

Sonya – Core S / Type 1 Learner

Sonya's main questions are, "Why should I learn this?" and, "Why is this important to me and/or those around me?" She values learning alongside others who share her desire for social interaction. Hers is a need for reflecting, sharing, and being able to relate to the content being learned. Although she enjoys personal involvement as she's introduced to new material, she doesn't veer too far into the risk of revealing too much of herself as she processes it. Sonya does best when she knows what's expected of her in advance. She likes feedback from others, and she'll rely on that as well as her personal intuition to guide her decisions for completing her work.

Carl – Core C / Type 2 Learner

Carl's main questions are, "What do the experts think about this?" and, "What other resources are available?" He wants to understand how new information is organized so he can analyze the concepts as a logical framework, or model. His is a need for analyzing information. He values both the details and the larger picture, and wants to understand both of those before taking any actions. He likes having lots of time to think about new learning before being quizzed on it. The more familiar Carl is with the data he has acquired, and the more familiar he is with the expected results (along with the timeline for achieving those results), the better he will be at making decisions for completing a project on time.

In the following four chapters, we'll explore each style with a bit more depth. By way of reminder, as you go through these chapters:

1. Identify your own tendencies and preferences
2. Identify the tendencies and preferences of your spouse
3. Identify the tendencies and preferences of your children

And, if you notice that your style is different from your spouse or children, prepare to adapt (as opposed to criticize).

NOTE: Feel free to skip over the chapters that don't apply if you don't have people in your family with that core style.

Chapter 6

Core D (Dominant) / Type 3 Learners

Marston called this type "Dominant" (D) because he found that one of the driving characteristics of people in this quadrant was to DOMINATE problems. When they encounter a difficulty, they see it as a challenge and they want to be victorious.

Core D / Type 3 Learners are:

Task-oriented / faster-paced when making decisions

Ambitious	Forceful	Decisive
Strong-Willed	Independent	Goal-Oriented

Core D / Type 3 Learner Motivations:

Do it NOW / WIN / Be in Charge

Ways to talk with a Core D / Type 3 learner include:

- Stay focused on the tasks at hand – not too much "fun" or chit chat
- Be brief and to the point – don't over-elaborate or provide too much detail; their eyes glaze over if you get into too much detail
- Be prepared and be well-organized – don't jump between topics

Core D / Type 3 Learners have a naturally strong desire to be in charge. If a core D is not the leader of a group be assured that he or she will be pushing the group along so he or she can "achieve results." This tendency also correlates with their strong need to have a challenge. Without a challenge, this style can quickly become bored.

Core D's usually like more risk than other styles are willing to accept. They also have a strong desire to win. Captain Kirk of *Star Trek* fame could easily be classified as having a Core D temperament. His need for challenge and his willingness to take risks enabled him to, "Boldly go where no man had gone before."

So you know, each style has an associated emotion. For the strong D the emotional is *anger*. Core D's tend to have a "short fuse" and are usually quick to get angry. By the same token, they also become UN-angry and "move on" just as quickly. Those that score low on the D-scale often take a long time to become angry, and in the same way, their anger tends to subside slowly over time.

In terms of communications, strong Core D / Type 3 Learners are direct and pointed, often forgoing tact and diplomacy so they can quickly get to their business.

Observable factors to help identify a core D individual include extroversion, being task-oriented, impatience with people, making quick decisions, making lots of changes, usually in a hurry to get somewhere, and setting many goals. They like to delegate but don't often take the time to give instructions when they delegate.

Additionally, Core D / Type 3 Learners can be identified by their self-starting capacity, their ability to push activities along so that deadlines are met, and their ability to focus on the possibilities. They also place a high value on time, are often the initiators in activities, and of the four styles, Core D / Type 3 Learners will be the ones most likely to challenge the status quo.

Options give Core D / Type 3 Learners a sense of control, which they like. Therefore, it is wise to give them choices! *NOTE*: It is best to make all the options you provide win/win!

How a Core D / Type 3 Learner might appear:

Donna, a homeschooled 3rd grader, didn't mind if adults read to her, but if her siblings read to her, she would become easily distracted. Donna struggled in math until she got a concept down, but once it was understood, she was like a math wizard. She also did well in science. However, it should be noted that she was also quite skilled at pushing her siblings out of the way so she could be front-row center during science experiments!

Donna loved working alone on projects and rarely wanted help. When she was asked to build something to represent a math concept, she jumped at the opportunity and completed the project in short order. She was very proud of herself whenever she solved any kind of problem.

After Donna was done with an assignment, she usually found a way to explain her learning as it applied to some practical task around the house.

Donna is a Type 3 learner. As a Type 3, she's a common-sense learner who prefers thinking and doing, often on her own. Type 3 learners are adept at solving problems, are drawn to how things work, and are quite comfortable with tasks and deadlines.

Best practices for teaching Core D / Type 3 Learners:

- Active problem solving
- Step-by-step procedures
- Touching, manipulating, and constructing
- Demonstrations, experimentation, tinkering, and competition

Know that Core D / Type 3 Learners prefer the following:

- Objective thinking & facts over ideas
- Summaries over details
- Opportunities to "win" / overcome a problem

PS. On a sad note, Donna's parents could not understand why Donna appeared so bossy to her siblings and why she preferred working alone. As Type 1 learners themselves, (both of them were DISC Core S), they thought something was wrong with their daughter. In their attempts to change her, they tried forcing her to verbally "reflect" on her thoughts and feelings (which she didn't like).

Donna's independence was viewed (incorrectly) by her parents as defiance. In fact, her parents even took her to a child psychologist thinking Donna might have oppositional defiance disorder. Bottom line, Donna's parents were NOT trying to understand their daughter. They erroneously thought their children should be miniature versions of themselves.

Core D / Type 3 Learners constitute 10-15% of the US population.

Chapter 7

Core I (Influencing) / Type 4 Learners

Marston called this type "Influencers" (I) because a driving characteristics of people in this quadrant is INFLUENCING others to their way of thinking. Core I / Type 4 learners enjoy being with people. They seek out and engage others, with fun being a common motivator.

Core I / Type 4 Learners are:

People-oriented / faster-paced when making decisions

Enthusiastic	Friendly	Demonstrative
Expressive	Confident	Spontaneous

Core I / Type 4 Learner Motivations:

Have FUN! EXPERIENCE LIFE!

Ways to talk with a Core I / Type 4 learner include:

- Be warm and friendly; Ask their opinion; Allow them time to talk
- Put details in writing; They're focused on relationships, therefore they like required tasks written down so they can remember them
- Keep the conversation going; Offer practical ideas for getting things done

Core I / Type 4 learners have a strong level of trust and naturally like interacting with others. Being liked and gaining approval is often very important to them. Core I's enjoy getting others excited about life, and for people who score very strongly in this category, the desire for experiencing excitement with others can often feel exaggerated to those who do not share this style.

Core I's express themselves very well and seek to enjoy all of life's experiences. Robin Williams, the late comedian and actor, was definitely a Core I. His outgoing, fun-loving, and gregarious persona allowed him to engage others no matter where he was or what he was doing. The character of Abby Scuito from *NCIS* is also a Core I.

The emotional factor for a Core I is optimism. Core I's tend to believe that even the most difficult things can be accomplished if enough people rally together. You can usually tell if someone has a low "I" score if they are often skeptical and pessimistic.

In terms of communications, strong I / Type 4 Learners are quick to think on their feet. Unfortunately, this skill allows them to come up with quick excuses for not following through on projects (which is often a result of their spending too much time socializing).

Additionally, core I's can be identified by their creative problem-solving ability, their positive sense of humor, and placing a high value on being a team-player. They're often good at negotiating conflict and articulating themselves verbally. They like talking about what interests them, their friends, and their goals. Remember, if details are to be communicated it is always best to present it in written form (checklists are best) so the core I's can refer to it later.

How a Core I / Type 4 Learner might appear:

All through his life, Ian liked having friends and spending time with them. In school, he loved "tinkering" with the whatever he could get his hands on, and when he had nothing but paperwork to do, school was not nearly exciting enough for him. In fact, it sometimes brought him to tears. He found himself extremely bored and taxed having to memorize facts for the sake of memorizing the facts. Memorization was much easier if he could relate the facts to the actions or intentions of specific people in history.

Ian had wonderful spontaneity, and when it took hold of him, he focused so intensely that he often lost track of time. This caused some problems with managing his studies, and sometimes he couldn't get his work done in a timely manner – much to the dismay of his parents.

Whenever possible, Ian preferred thinking outside the box. For example, instead of preparing a report on the Viet Nam war out of his history book, he asked to interview a neighbor who had fought in the war to get his insights and opinions. He then presented his findings by creating display boards with lots of pictures and telling his neighbor's stories. When given an option, anything "hands-on" was Ian's choice.

Ian is a Type 4 learner. As such, he's a dynamic learner who favors creating things (and ideas) and incorporating some form of physical activity. Type 4 Learners are comfortable with newness, change, and taking risks. It's not uncommon for them to learn best by trial and error, introducing new factors to influence different outcomes.

Best practices for teaching Core I / Type 4 Learners:

- Lots of interaction with others
- Opportunities to challenge the status quo
- Freedom from rigid routines
- Have a method for writing down tasks & expectations

Know that Core I / Type 4 Learners prefer the following:

- Creative problem-solving
- Fast-moving, stimulating conversation
- Positive, upbeat learning environments

NOTE: Research indicates that the overwhelming majority of high school dropouts are Type 4 Learners. This is because institutional schools are not set up to accommodate learners who prefer learning via the above-described methods, and Type 4's can easily get bored with rote academics. When that happens, if Type 4 Learners do not feel like they fit in, they are more likely than the other three styles to move on to something else.

Core I / Type 4 Learners constitute 25-30% of the US population.

Chapter 8
Core S (Steady) / Type 1 Learners

Marston called this type "Steady" (S) because a driving characteristics of people in this quadrant is a STEADINESS in their pace. Core S / Type 1 learners are not fond of unannounced change, and prefer completing one task before moving on to another. This type also dislikes conflict.

Core S / Type 1 Learners are:
People-oriented / slower-paced when making decisions

Patient	Reliable	Steady
Relaxed	Predictable	Modest

Core S / Type 1 Learner Motivations:
PEACE & LOYALTY

Ways to talk with a Core S / Type 1 learner include:

- Be personable; Show sincere interest in their perspective
- Talk softly and non-threateningly; Watch their body language for signs of disagreement
- Give them time to think when asking for a decision; Minimize risk whenever possible

Core S / Type 1 learners are very loyal, patient, peace-loving, and relaxed. They have a natural desire to work steadily and quietly to help get projects completed. Rather than having many friends (like

Core I / Type 4 learners), Core S's prefer fewer relationships, and desire for them to be deeper and long-term. They are practical and patient, doing what needs to be done so a job is completed. Core S's prefer to finish one project before starting another.

Core S's do not like conflict. They shy away from it and avoid it wherever possible. One famous Core S is Mr. Rogers. He was always steady and loyal, desiring to know people in long-term relationships. He never let his emotions get out of control, he was a great listener, and he showed everyone patience and empathy. He was also dependable, and a logical, step-wise thinker.

The emotional factor for an S is non-emotion. This is not to say that this style does not have emotions – they do, it's just that they tend not to display them. Think of the phrase, "Still waters run deep." You could also say that Core S's usually have a good poker face, as it can be hard to tell via body language when they agree or disagree with you. Conversely, people scoring low on the S scale tend to wear their hearts on their sleeves.

In terms of communications, strong S / Type 1 Learners are "indirect," meaning they don't like to confront others directly with a problem. If you sense hesitancy, it's best to state that and ask them if they have any concerns. Secondly, Core S types like taking their time when making decisions. And, because they don't like change, it's best to provide them plenty of lead time before implementing a change, and, if possible, get their input on how to implement the change.

Observable factors to help identify core S's include introversion, being people-oriented, and leaning towards more traditional ways of doing things. They enjoy a relaxed pace, are usually tolerant of other behavioral extremes, and work well when they have daily "to-do" lists. They tend to be a little on the sloppy side, and they enjoy short-term goals that have low-risk factors. Helping them set priorities will speed things up. They tend to see everything as high priority, and then get stuck trying to decide which to do first.

Core S / Type 1 Learners like seeing the personal application or meaning in their learning. Forcing them to stay on the academic side may cause disengagement and a slowdown in an S's motivation to learn.

How a Core S / Type 1 Learner might appear:

Sonya was in 5th grade when she decided she didn't like math. She'd enjoyed learning up until then. She did fine with language, reading, spelling, science and history. And, everyone noticed that her poetry was quite good. However, for Sonya, math was a problem. She couldn't find any practical application for it, and the patterns and algorithms seemed like so much busy work. Math was like a huge black hole to her. Then, after she got to junior high and was tasked with learning algebra, she wanted to quit.

Sonya's parents were confused about what to do, until one day when the subject came up while visiting extended family. Sonya's aunt listened and then thoughtfully said, "You know, your poetry is excellent. I think you are going to do very well in algebra."

Sonya was confused. "How do you figure?" she said. "Poetry is right brain, math is left. I'm not sure the left side of my brain is working." Her aunt smiled and answered, "Poetry is all about symmetry, and so is algebra. You could think of algebra as the symmetrical balancing board of math." As Sonya pondered this, two things happened. First she realized someone important to her outside of her normal learning circle was seeing a bigger picture, and that person believed that algebra was important. She wanted to see that bigger picture, too. Second, she started looking for the symmetry that her aunt was talking about. And, when she found it, she resonated with it.

Sonya is a Type 1 learner. As a Type 1, she is highly imaginative, caring, and spends much time reflecting on how the things she's learning impact her life and the lives of those around her.

Always watch body language on Core S / Type 1 Learners, because if they disagree with something, they are not likely to say anything. This is due to their dislike for confrontation. If you see them clamming up, draw them out by asking a gentle question about their thoughts or concerns, then give them time to formulate their thoughts.

Best practices for teaching Core S / Type 1 Learners:

- When decisions are required, give them time to think
- Give them a road map to follow
- Small, regular groups where relationships can develop
- Keep the number of assignments small and manageable

Know that Core S / Type 1 Learners prefer the following:

- Sincere, casual, personable instruction
- Opportunities to brainstorm and explore relationships
- Encouragement instead of criticism

Core S / Type 1 Learners constitute 30-35% of the US population.

Chapter 9
Core C (Compliant) / Type 2 Learners

Marston called this type "Compliant" (C) because a driving characteristics of people in this quadrant is a naturally strong desire to follow procedures. They believe rules have been created for a reason, and want hard data before agreeing to make changes.

Core C / Type 2 Learners are:

Task-oriented / slower-paced when making decisions

Systematic	Accurate	Patient
Perfectionistic	Careful	Conventional

Core C / Type 2 Learner Motivations:

Do it RIGHT

Ways to talk with a Core C / Type 2 learner include:

- Prepare your material in advance; Take time to be thorough
- Stick to business; Have an action plan that includes dates and specific goals; Be systematic in reviewing that plan
- Be accurate and realistic; Give them time to think so they can analyze facts; Keep emotions to a minimum

Core C / Type 2 learners are very loyal and prefer taking whatever time is needed to complete tasks with detailed precision. The character Mr. Spock from the *Star Trek* series is a good example of this. Mr. Spock emphasized logic, was highly accurate, and perfectionistic. His character is emotionally detached, and people scoring very strongly in the C scale can also appear the same way.

The emotional factor for the Core C is fear. To be more specific, Core C / Type 2 Learners are very aware of the consequences for not following procedures, and want to avoid those consequences. Conversely, people scoring low on the C scale tend to show little or no concern for bending or breaking rules. *NOTE*: A strong Core C / Type 2 Learner who has a corresponding low "I" (Influencing) score will usually come across as quite skeptical.

In terms of communications, strong C types are direct but relatively non-emotional. Observable factors include introversion and leaning towards a critical approach to information and/or procedures. They are very concerned about how change will affect the status quo, and are usually reserved with respect to body language, using few, if any, gestures. Core C's may avoid conflict, especially when they are not confident of their knowledge about the matter at hand.

Additionally, core C's can be identified by their objective thinking and maintaining high standards as they conscientiously pursue information to fulfill their assigned tasks. They tend to be diplomatic and can be intrigued by even the smallest of details.

Teaching Core C / Type 2 Learners means being straightforward, direct, and emotion-free. They like to see action plans in writing, complete with deadlines and mid-course progress assessments. Being vague about what is expected will cause tension, as will forcing them to make quick decisions. Take time to cover what needs to be covered, but don't veer off track. If a core C disagrees with you, provide data and facts from a respected source.

Like a Core S, Core C individuals need time to adjust to changes.

How a Core C / Type 2 Learner might appear:

When Carl knew what was going to happen and what was expected of him, he thrived, especially if those activities were written down in a linear, logical outline. Details were never a bother for him, and finding the answer to a question often served as a springboard for even more questions. When he received complex Lego projects or plastic models for his birthday, Carl would patiently and diligently read through each detail and work to ensure the kit was assembled according to the instructions.

Carl was also drawn to solving puzzles and deciphering logic problems, and he loved books. He would spend hours pouring over the details of a book on airplane schematics or the facts outlined in a book on nature. If you gave Carl a book filled with facts and data, he would be quite content to sit for hours while pouring over the details of the book's content.

Carl is a Type 2 learner. He's the stereotypical analytic student who favors reflecting and thinking. Type 2 learners enjoy acquiring knowledge. They can conceptualize new ideas, analyze and classify their experiences and organize ideas; are highly organized and at home with details and data; are good at step-by-step tasks; are fascinated with structure; believe in their ability to understand; and are committed to making the world more lucid.

Best practices for teaching Core C / Type 2 Learners:

- Solo work / few or no group activities
- Provide a syllabus or an outline of "what-is-due-when"
- Stick to factual discussions, not emotional ones
- Reassure them when they are doing the job right

Know that Core C / Type 2 Learners prefer the following:

- Information and data to analyze
- Time to analyze problems from many angles
- Time to think before answering

Students like Carl enjoy objective thinking, reflection before action, and what some might call "impersonal" learning (where they don't have to get involved personally with the subject matter). Type 2 Learners are quite conceptual and are not fans of experiential learning, especially as they perceive (take in) new concepts.

Core C / Type 2 Learners constitute 20-25% of the US population.

Chapter 10
Left-Brain / Right-Brain Learners

By the time most folks have finished high school, they've at least heard about the terms "left-brained" and "right-brained." And while many have heard about it, not everyone has had the opportunity to learn how left- and right-brain styles influence learning. Therefore, since this is a book about becoming a student of your students, we thought it would be a good idea to include the differences on brain hemisphericity. In fact, if you're going to be a student of your student, learning about this is pretty necessary.

It's one thing to know if someone is a Type 1, 2, 3, or 4 learner, but in her work developing the 4MAT System (a method for creating classroom curriculum that reaches all four learning styles), Bernice McCarthy realized that differentiating among the four styles was not enough. To truly reach learners where they were, brain modality had to be included. And so, we include a chapter on it!

First, a little background. Starting in the middle of the 20th century, a neurobiologist by the name of Roger W. Sperry spearheaded research into what the different sides of the brain do. He knew that the brain had two distinct hemispheres connected by a nerve bundle called the corpus callosum, and that those nerve fibers facilitated communication between the two hemispheres. But he wanted to know which sides of the brain were responsible for different aspects of our memory and our behavior. (And, we can also say, our learning.) Sperry's research revealed that each side of brain is "pre-wired" to perceive and process different types of information.

Further research has found that in some people, the left-side of the brain is more dominant, and in other people, the right side is more dominant. The neurological term used when talking about right-brain or left-brain dominance is *hemisphericity*. However, you should know that hemisphericity is not an "either/or" proposition. Some people are VERY left-brain, while others only *tend* to that direction. The same goes for the right. And still others have relatively balanced tendencies. Those with balanced preferences are usually referred to as "whole-brained," but this doesn't mean the person is more complete. It only indicates a flexibility in his/her ability to perceive and process new data.

That said, most geniuses are either heavily left or heavily right. For example, top-rated musicians, designers, and artists tend to be strongly right-brained, whereas top-rated mathematicians, programmers, and scientists tend to be very left-brained.

According to the left-brain, right-brain dominance theory, the right side of the brain is wired for expressive and creative tasks, and the left-side of the brain is wired for tasks that involve logic, language and analytical thinking. In a nutshell, the fundamental differences in hemisphericity are shown below. As you read them, first try to identify your own preferences, then those of your spouse, then those of your students (remember, it's important to "know thyself" first):

Left-Brain Dominant is often better at:	Right-Brain Dominant is often better at:
Language	Music
Logic	Expressing emotions
Critical thinking	Intuition
Numbers	Colors
Reasoning	Creativity

If you want a better idea as to the strength of your pre-wired preferences, we suggest taking several of the many free online left-brain / right-brain assessments. (Search online for "Hemispheric Dominance Test" or "right brain left brain test.") The reason we suggest taking several of them is that free online assessments may or may not be created by professionals, so the results may give you an idea, but won't be exactly accurate. The more you take, the better of an idea you'll have as to your preference.

If you're willing to spend a few dollars for a well-respected and accurate assessment, we recommend the *Hemispheric Mode Indicator*, available for $11.50 (at the time of this writing). It can be found online at aboutlearning.com. (*NOTE*: we don't earn any royalties by making this recommendation, but we've used the assessment before and trust the results.)

As a general rule, if a person is predominately left-brained, he or she is typically perceived as:

- intellectual
- geeky or nerdy
- introverted
- rule-oriented
- uncomfortable with unstructured play

As a general rule, if a person is predominately right-brained, he or she is typically perceived as:

- emotional
- intuitive
- relational
- social
- comfortable with improvisation and unstructured play

First you'll want to determine your own hemispheric preference. Then identify the hemisphericity of your student(s). Finally, clearly identify differences (if any). Know that you'll want to teach in the style that's most comfortable to you. However, what's comfortable for you will not be comfortable for your students if their hemisphericity is very different from yours.

If you find a large gap, it is up to you to adapt to your students. You cannot expect your students to adapt to your teaching preference.

Teaching to Right-Brain dominant children:

Strong right-brained students often struggle with traditional learning methods. This is not because being right-brained is a disability (it's NOT), it's because most curriculum is created by (and for) left-brained learners! Workbooks, worksheets, lectures, and fact-memorization are not seen as fun by right-brain learners. To right-brained folks, those methods of learning can be quite taxing. Heather, an 11-year old right-learner, absolutely hated math worksheets. She even despised word searches and crossword puzzles.

In right-brain dominant people, learning tends to occur in wholes rather than in parts. In other words, right-brain learners can readily grasp concepts, but often struggle with details. It would be great if we could get through life on concepts alone, but details are necessary.

So, how do we help right-brain learners get needed details?

One answer is to help make the details creative. For example, spelling is a necessary skill, but much of it is rote memorization. To make spelling creative, one parent gave her daughter some pipe cleaners and had her "create" the word by bending the pipe cleaner into the correct spelling of the word. Another parent gave her son some modelling clay, and let him roll the clay into long, spaghetti-type lengths, and then spell the words using the rolled clay.

Still another parent did a pre-test on the spelling words, and then wrote out the letters that the child got correct on a 3x5 card, leaving spaces for the letters that were incorrect. Then her son could choose colored markers to fill in the correct letters, and even draw pictures to help him remember what those correct letter were supposed to be.

For example, when her son misspelled the word *because* as bekawse, she wrote be__a__se on a 3x5 card. He looked up the correct spelling of the word, and then used a blue marker to write the "c" and drew some water around it as a mental reminder (a homonym mnemonic of the word "sea"). Then he chose a different marker and wrote the letter "u" in its proper space, and drew a lamb to indicate a "ewe" for a homonym mnemonic. By deciding to use those creative visuals, the "rote" memorization became more creative and colorful!

Believe it or not, written composition can also be a chore for right-brained learners. Linear outlines can feel too restrictive, thus blocking the free flow of ideas that are itching to make their way out of a right-brain student's head. One solutions for this is to teach "spider graphing," which is sometimes called "mind mapping." If you're unfamiliar with the concept, a quick Internet search will provide examples. But even for extreme right-brain learners, spider graphing can feel too limiting, or even confusing. Therefore, be sure to show your learner how to use the spider graphing technique to first collect and record important ideas, and place them in a logical order. For those scoring strongly in right-brain hemisphericity, be sure to practice spider graphing a LOT on very simple subjects that are already familiar to the learner. The more you do of this, the easier it will be for them to "see" how it works. Don't be afraid to use different colors for different phases of a created outline, as well as for separating primary and secondary ideas.

Math can be a difficult subject for right-brain learners, too, because it is usually thought of (and taught) as logic. However, through the use of stories and colors and pictures, math is made easier for right-brain learners. For example, many right-brain learners have difficulty with assigning place value. But, but using different colors for the different places (10's, 100's, etc.), a right-brain learner will "get it" much faster.

For basic math facts, telling stories and drawing pictures as you go will help learners "see" the processes.

As you can tell from these examples, getting creative solutions for right-brain learners is not expensive. However, if you're a left-brain learner, it will require much "outside the box" thinking. In fact, if you are strongly left-brained, you may have a difficult time seeing a value in all this creativity needed just to learn facts. To you, it's just facts, and facts are easy. But to right-brain learners, memorizing facts is like walking through knee-deep mud. It can be a huge frustration, and even physically painful as the brain struggles to process things, even to the point of tears.

Therefore, don't be afraid to experiment with creative, colorful, musical, and even emotional ways to help your right-brain learners process new information. The more the learner can visualize and have an opportunity to be creative with projects and assignments, the better.

Teaching to Left-Brain dominant children:

If you find your student is left-brain dominant, just think "traditional schooling" and you're pretty close to the mark for successful learning techniques. Left-brain learners love outlines, worksheets, and rote memorization, so give them outlines, worksheets, and facts to memorize. And, they will usually enjoy crossword puzzles, listening to lectures, and taking timed tests to assess their learning, so provide those, too.

When introducing new material, present a big picture along with a couple of discussion questions. Left-Brain learners often enjoy contemplating and dialoging on large, abstract concepts.

For assignments to help left-brain students process their newly acquired data, individual assignments work best. As students get older, you can have them write research papers that require them to compare and contrast what they've just learned to something they've learned previously. This helps cement their new learning.

When it comes to learning environments, noise is usually frustrating and distracting for left-brain learners, so, if possible, provide a quiet place for them to learn.

Chapter 11
Multiple Intelligences

Although some readers may have been already familiar with DISC Assessments and how they relate to learning styles, and even more may have been aware of right-brain/left-brain differences, we have found that not too many parents are aware of the concept of multiple intelligences.

By way of background information, the theory of people having multiple intelligences is different from what we commonly refer to as IQ (intelligence quotient). The multiple intelligence theory emerged in the 1980's, based on research spearheaded by Howard Gardner at the Harvard Graduate School of Education. According to Gardner's theory, intelligence goes beyond standardized IQ tests, which mostly measure a person's ability to work with visual shapes, mathematical problems, language, and cognitive recall. One might say, "Well, those four areas cover a lot," but Gardner proposes that one's intellect goes beyond those traditional measures.

In fact, Gardner suggests that all human beings have at least nine different areas of intelligence. Furthermore, he suggests that in each individual, several of these areas will be dominant, some will be "average," and some will be diminished, or not significant players. The nine areas of intelligence identified by Gardner are:

Verbal-Linguistic Intelligence. People with strong intelligence in this area have well-developed verbal skills and sensitivity to the sounds, the meanings, and the rhythm of words.

Mathematical-Logical Intelligence. People with strong intelligence in this area have an innate ability to think conceptually and abstractly, with a strong capacity to discern logical or numerical patterns.

Musical Intelligence. People with strong intelligence in this area have an ability to understand and appreciate rhythm, pitch and timber. They are often adept at creating music, as well.

Visual-Spatial Intelligence. People with strong intelligence in this area have a capacity to think in images and pictures, as well as to visualize things in their mind both accurately (concretely) and abstractly (conceptually).

Bodily-Kinesthetic Intelligence. People with strong intelligence in this area have an ability to control their own body movements, and also to handle / manipulate objects skillfully.

Interpersonal Intelligence. People with strong intelligence in this area have a capacity to detect and respond appropriately to the moods, motivations and desires of others.

Intrapersonal Intelligence. People with strong intelligence in this area have a capacity to easily tune into their inner feelings, values, beliefs, and thinking processes. In other words, they are quite self-aware.

Naturalistic Intelligence. People with strong intelligence in this area have an ability to recognize, relate to and systematize things in nature, such as plants, animals, and other natural objects.

Existential Intelligence. Gardner named this category "existential" because he didn't want to get into spiritual things, but that is exactly what is measured in this category. People with strong intelligence in this area have a desire and capacity to tackle deep questions about human existence and the meaning of life.

As with all of what we present in this book, remember to "know thyself" first. We recommend doing an Internet search for "Multiple Intelligence Test." (One good free assessment can be found at literacynet.org.) If your child is old enough, you can have him/her take one, too. If the child is too young, you can assist and explain each question along the way.

However, if your child is just way too young, you can still become familiar with the nine categories and then observe your child. Look for how he/she lines up with the nine different categories. Most people will have two or three strong aptitudes that stand out, so with a little observation and thinking, you should be able to get a rough idea of where your child's interests lie.

So, whether your child is four or fourteen, you can look for the following behaviors as clues for which areas might be your child's stronger intelligences.

Examples of Identifiable Clues

Eight-year old David is gifted at assembling model ships and airplanes and seems to be a born tree-climber. He also loves doing role plays and acting in skits. With that, we can start looking deeper to see if he has innate intelligence in Bodily / Kinesthetic.

As for 6-year old Eva, she sings with beautiful pitch and seems to pick up melodies and rhythms naturally. She can also tell you when instruments are out of tune. Chances are she has a strong Musical intelligence.

Whenever Russell picks up a pencil, he starts drawing realistic scenes. He's also very good at reading maps and loves photography. It's likely that Russell is strong in Visual / Spatial intelligence.

Simon loves doing science experiments and thinks it's fun to solve math puzzles in his head. Memorizing his multiplication table was a snap. Here we could deduce that Simon is strong in Logical / Mathematical.

Seven-year old Anna loves to read. And we mean LOVES to read. Also, she regularly asks what different words mean when she hears adults using them. Chances are that Anna has strong Verbal / Linguistic intelligence.

Olivia just seems to "get" people. At 12, she is the person that her friends turn to when they need an ear. She reads their body language well, and helps her friends see things from different perspectives. It's likely that Olivia has strong Interpersonal intelligence.

Carl can tell you all about birds and their nesting habits. He loves camping and hiking and exploring along creeks and rivers. It's probable that Carl has strong Naturalist intelligence.

Katilyn is known for seeing the big picture on many things. She enjoys being outside, and asks a lot of questions about life. Discussions about religions are always of interest to her. It's likely that Katilyn has an innate Existential (Spiritual) intelligence.

Nine-year old Hailey keeps a diary and enjoys spending time alone, appearing introverted. She is self-motivated, but prefers working independently. It's possible that Hailey has a strong Intrapersonal intelligence.

Remember, all humans possess all nine intelligences, but each will vary in its intensity. Also, each one of us has two or three of these that are stronger than the rest. Therefore, because each person has a different arrangement of intellectual composition, can you see how these different combinations add to the uniqueness of each person?

Now that you have an understanding of the nine different intelligences and some of the behaviors that each one might display, the following list provides some activities you can do to help your student enjoy his or her learning:

Verbal-Linguistic Intelligence:

- Have students read books, articles, and papers on the subject matter
- Provide word games such as crossword puzzles & word searches on the subject matter
- Have students write stories, reports, or poems about the material and give presentations
- Hold "discussion groups" on various subjects

Mathematical-Logical Intelligence:

- Assign students to collect & organize items related to the lesson
- Look for patterns in things (such as poetry, music, art, & history)
- Do "proofs" by solving problems in more than one way
- Let kids create experiments that validate a concept

Musical Intelligence:

- Incorporate music into lessons
- Research the types of music popular in the time period of history or social studies
- Encourage students to write songs about what they're learning
- Have students find topic-related songs on YouTube (or similar)

Visual-Spatial Intelligence:

- Encourage students to keep a "visual journal" in which they keep images representing their learning
- Use spider graphs (mind maps) to teach and/or review material
- Have students create drawings or a photo exhibit on subject matter
- Have students create or put together jigsaw or 3-D puzzles (e.g., Legos or clay) on subject matter

Bodily-Kinesthetic Intelligence:

- Use manipulatives; let student play with objects related to the subject
- Do act-it-out (for literature) and/or role-play
- Plan field trips that reinforce subject matter
- Have students create/build models of anything in their lesson

Interpersonal Intelligence:

- Assign group projects whenever possible
- Encourage students to interview people who are specialists in the area being studied
- Assign students to teach others a portion of the subject matter
- Incorporate community service activities where possible and where applicable

Intrapersonal Intelligence:

- Teach students how to use spider graphs (mind maps)
- In history, talk about what it must have been like to be an individual from a period being studied
- Encourage daily/weekly journaling on personal thoughts/concerns
- Have students write reflections on topics studied in class

Naturalistic Intelligence:

- When weather permits and when it's practical, hold class outside
- Write and/or perform skits involving things found in nature
- Where possible, show how nature and/or weather affects what is being studied
- Have the student keep a nature journal

Existential / Spiritual Intelligence:

- Provide overviews so the student can see the big picture
- Have students examine learning from different points of view
- At the end of each lesson, have students summarize learning
- Have students teach others what they've learned
- Discuss how the topic being learned relates to the world overall

The above list is only an abbreviated starting point. As you become more of a student of your students, you are encouraged to dig deeper and learn more about how to help your child excel in his or her natural giftings (aka intelligences).

By the way, we should also present Gardner's overall definition of intelligence (which we find quite useful). According to Gardner, Intelligence is the capacity to solve [real world] problems and fashion products.

In other words, the nine intelligences are not merely ways to help a child perceive and process information (although they help immensely in that capacity). When it comes to solving problems and/or fashioning products, your child will likely excel in whatever areas your child has innate, natural intelligence. Keep that in mind in your endeavor to, "Train up a child in the way he should go."

Chapter 12
Cognitive Measures: The MBTI - Part 1

Whereas DISC assessments measure behavior and Multiple Intelligences measure natural, innate intellect, the Myers-Briggs Type Indicator (MBTI) is a tool for assessing four cognitive measures (which MBTI practitioners call *psychological preferences*).

In this chapter we'll cover the four spectrums measured by the MBTI, descriptions that we typically see at each end of the spectrums, and tips for how to teach to people who are strong one way or the other on any of the four spectrums.

We should note that the *Keirsey Temperament Sorter* is a very close cousin to the MBTI, and either assessment will provide you with similar insights. More on that in the next chapter.

What the MBTI Measures

The MBTI can get complex quickly with "dominant functions" and "auxiliary functions," but the purpose of this chapter is not to get you certified but rather provide useful, essential understandings.

Like the DISC assessment, the cognitive measures in the MBTI rely on four spectrums. Those spectrums measure multiple things, but fundamentally they look at:

- How we receive and direct energy
- How we perceive information
- How we process information
- How we make decisions

At this point you may be wondering, "Wait, weren't the DISC profile / Learning Styles determined using how we perceive and process information? If so, how is this different?" To that we say, "Great observation," and here's how they differ:

DISC profiles and Learning Styles measure how we perceive and process *behaviorally*. The MBTI considers how we perceive and process *mentally*.

Bear with us as we first explain the preferences in the MBTI spectrums. We'll give some examples of the perceiving/processing differences in the next chapter.

How we Receive and Direct Energy

The first scale (or spectrum) in the MBTI shows our preference for how we receive and direct energy. The two ends of the spectrum are called *Extraversion* and *Introversion*. You may be accustomed to using a particular definition for each of those words, but so that we're on the same page, the MBTI uses those terms to identify people who prefer "outward turning" (extravert) or "inward turning" (introvert).

People are on the ***Extravert*** side of the Energy spectrum if they prefer to be on teams, have lots of friends, and know lots of people. They are "people" people, seen as outgoing, and sometimes impulsive. In fact, being around other people seems to energize them, and they redirect that energy into the situations and people they're with. When it comes to learning, they like knowing a little bit about a lot of different things. They tend to get re-energized by being around other people.

People are on the ***Introvert*** side of the Energy spectrum if they prefer being alone and doing things by themselves, or with one or two others they trust. Rather than know a lot of people, they prefer knowing fewer people, and knowing them very well. They are reserved individuals who are not quick to act without much consideration. Because being around people requires energy to be directed outward, Introverts get re-energized by being alone. When it comes to learning, they like to ponder ideas quietly and deeply. They tend to get re-energized by being alone.

Obviously, some people score in the middle of this spectrum, which means two things: First, it's harder to peg their preference, because they receive and direct energy situationally. Second, they can adapt fairly easily to many different people and situations.

Take a moment and try to identify which side of the "Energy" spectrum your student prefers, or if he scores near the middle.

How we Perceive Information

The second spectrum in the MBTI shows our preference for how we perceive information, or, more specifically, what *kind* of information we notice. The two ends of the spectrum are called *Sensing* and *Intuition*.

People are on the ***Sensing*** side of the Perceiving spectrum if they are first concerned with what they can physically sense around them. Whatever they can see, hear, touch, taste, and smell is real. Thus, they are attuned to notice the actual circumstances around them, i.e., whatever they are experiencing in the present. They trust accurate descriptions over symbolism, but can sometimes get so caught up in the facts that they fail to see the possibilities those facts represent. When it comes to education, Sensors prefer being able to use whatever they're learning.

People are on the ***Intuition*** side of the Perceiving spectrum if they are first concerned with the patterns and implications of what they are taking in. Their focus is on future possibilities. Thus, they are adept at "reading between the lines" and seeing a bigger picture than what is currently before them. They often trust the symbolism within a topic over the facts of a matter, and can sometimes get so caught up in thinking about possibilities that they fail to make those possibilities a reality. When it comes to education, Intuitives prefer contemplating and thinking through whatever they're learning.

Again, some people score toward the middle of this spectrum, which means they perceive new information more holistically, sensing reality and perceiving possibilities rather equally. Take a moment and try to identify which side of the spectrum your student prefers, or if he is more toward the middle.

How we Process Information

The third spectrum in the MBTI is about our preference for *processing* information, and the two ends of the spectrum are called *Thinking* and *Feeling.* Many MBTI practitioners say this spectrum is about making decisions. Reading their rationale, we see why they say that, but we believe this spectrum is more about how we process information *en route to making decisions.* Therefore, we'll stick with our term and say this spectrum measures how we *process* information.

Also, know that the monikers of Thinking and Feeling are not about having/not having thoughts or feelings. These are merely the terms Isabel Myers and Katharine Cook Briggs came up with for describing the two ends of this spectrum. You'll see why in just a minute, but know for sure that Thinkers feel and Feelers think!

People are on the ***Thinking*** side of the Processing spectrum if they evaluate information logically, technically, and scientifically. Truth far outweighs tact for Thinkers, because facts are facts, and they believe the only fair way to evaluate information is by weighing the facts. People are often subjective and illogical, so their personal desires—and even the Thinker's own desires—are rarely considered in the processing of data. In terms of education, Thinkers analyze pros and cons and prefer logical, unemotional interactions.

People are on the ***Feeling*** side of the Processing spectrum if they contemplate information from a human value perspective, with strong considerations made for harmony and compassion. Truth is important for Feelers, but it's vital that truth be communicated tactfully. Feelers believe people are at the heart of life, and just because hard truth exists doesn't mean it has to be communicated harshly. Facts by themselves are often cold and uncaring. In terms of education, Feelers are concerned about what is best for the people involved in the learning process.

Remember, some people will score toward the middle of this spectrum. When they do, it means they weigh facts and the needs of people rather equally. Take a moment and try to identify which side of the spectrum your student prefers, or if he is more toward the middle.

How we Make Decisions

The fourth spectrum in the MBTI is about our preference for *making decisions,* and the two ends of the spectrum are called *Judging* and *Perceiving*. MBTI practitioners say this spectrum is about *structure*. We agree that the spectrum assesses how one structures his decision as he moves through life, but with that, we think the differences are better understood as a *decision-making* spectrum.

Also, know that the term *Judging* does not mean one is judgmental. It was chosen to correlate to the role of a judge in a courtroom, whose job it is to make decisions and move on.

People are on the ***Judging*** side of the Decision-Making spectrum if they like it when things are decided. They are uncomfortable when decisions are not made, because then things are "up in the air," which is unsettling. Because of this mental framework, Judgers appear task-oriented and often have clearly written "to-do" lists. Their motto is, "Work, then play," because they are not fans of rushing at the last minute to get things done – they like things under control.

People are on the ***Perceiving*** side of the Decision-Making spectrum if they prefer delaying decisions and keeping their options open. They are uncomfortable when decisions are made, because firm decisions restrict any flexibility that may become necessary. With this mental framework, Perceivers appear loose and casual, keeping plans to a minimum. Their motto is, "Play, then, if required, work and play." They like staying uncommitted so they can respond to situations as conditions change, without having to undo a previous decision.

When people score toward the middle of this spectrum, it often means they know when decisions are needed quickly, when they are not, and the situations for when each approach is needed. Take a moment to identify which side of the spectrum your student prefers, or if he is more toward the middle.

Education Tips for MBTI Types

Extraverts love "thinking out loud" with others. The more people interaction, the better. *NOTE*: Be sure to inform your Extravert to

Value the Differences. Specifically, help them realize that not all people are Extraverts, and dragging Introverts into discussions will often cause discomfort for the Introvert.

Introverts love independent work, preferably in a quiet place. They prefer having access to multiple lines of information so they can study subjects in-depth, and time to think when asked a question.

Sensors prefer hands-on, relevant learning that is tied to real-world situations. They want to know what is expected of them, and do best when all the facts of a matter are presented in an ordered manner to form a foundation. *NOTE*: Be sure to assist your Sensor in seeing the bigger picture and the possibilities that exist in any given situation.

Intuitives like opportunities to be original when solving problems. They also like choices in their assignments. Once they learn a concept or skill, it's easy for Intuitives to become bored and want to move on to learning something else. *NOTE*: Be sure to assist your Intuitives to see the value of keeping an eye on the practical.

Thinkers, like Sensors, prefer to have material presented in a logical order. They relish feedback from others on their specific accomplishments. Thinkers will also desire that all students be treated fairly and that no one gets special treatment. *NOTE*: Help Thinkers see the human side of situations!

Feelers are more devoted to their work when they have relationships with their instructors and peers. They like feedback that's specific and positive, and when corrections must be made, they should be constructive, not done with personal criticism. *NOTE*: Help Feelers see things more from a practical, objective point-of-view.

Judgers want clear, concise, and consistent structure. They love having a plan with milestones and deadlines explained, as they are not fans of surprises. A Judger believes instructors must follow their syllabus and return graded papers when promised.

Perceivers want choices and options throughout their assignments. For them, learning is not just about a what, but a why. Therefore, they want to understand the reasons for the assignments they're given. Perceivers do not mind variety and spontaneity.

Chapter 13
Cognitive Measures: The MBTI - Part 2

We like the MBTI because it examines cognitive processes that are not readily observable. When two people score at the same end of a spectrum, or near the middle, they're going to get along okay with regard to what's measured on that spectrum (be it Energy, Perceiving, Processing, or Decisions).

However, if two people score at opposite ends of a spectrum, head-butting and/or internal angst and frustration is quite possible – and highly probable. But, an understanding of MBTI will make you aware of the potential hiccups, so you, as the parent, can stretch out and make accommodations for your learner.

Take, for example, a parent who is a strong Sensor, and a student who is a strong Intuitive. To the parent, the student appears illogical and driven by silly emotions. To the student, the parent is cold-hearted and not understanding. It is not the student's responsibility to adapt to the teacher, so in these differences, it's incumbent on the parent to either adapt his approach to teaching, or bring in some form of assistance to create an environment more conducive to learning for the student.

Let's also consider a parent who scores very strongly in Judging, but has a student who scores strongly in Perceiving. Without knowledge of this spectrum in the MBTI, the parent might easily (and incorrectly) determine that his student is lazy or inept, simply because the student puts off making decisions. However, with knowledge of how Judgers and Perceivers make decisions, the parent can make adjustments and equip his student with a framework that enables good learning, all while letting the student be who God made him to be.

Bottom line, as students of our students, if we have a child who scores strongly on one end of any of the MBTI spectrums, it helps us know more about what kind of learning environment to create so we can educate that child according to his way.

Things We Don't Like About the MBTI

As we mentioned at the beginning of the previous chapter, the MBTI can get complex quickly. For example, whether someone is an Extravert or Introvert impacts how they display their Sensor or Intuitive tendencies, and whether someone is a Judger or Perceiver plays out in either their Perceiving preference OR their Processing preference, depending on whether they are a Judger or a Perceiver.

Unlike other assessments mentioned in this book, the MBTI's spectrums are so interdependent they can be too complex to be fully useful without becoming a devout student of the assessment. That said, we think it's valuable to understand the spectrums measured in the assessment (or we wouldn't have included them in this book!).

Also, while the MBTI works very well at identifying people who score strongly at either end of the spectrum, the assessment doesn't help much for people who are more "even-keeled," scoring at or near the middle of any spectrum. Especially if the student is near the middle on all four spectrums!

For example, we struggle with "labeling" anyone as a *Thinker* if they're Thinker 53 percent of the time and Feeler 47 percent of the time, yet that's what the letter separations force us to do. The descriptions of a Thinker don't vary according to the intensity of one's score, so a "mild" Thinker gets described the same as someone who's a very strong Thinker. We think that lack of distinction can interfere with making good use of someone's MBTI scores.

As for how that plays out, take a person who's near the middle, but just *barely* an ENFP right down the line. Now consider someone else who is *barely* an ISTJ right down the line. In actual makeup, hardly any difference exists between the two of them, but the letter designations make it look like they're polar opposites.

Correlations to DISC

On the surface, it's easy to think that direct correlations automatically exist between certain aspects of MBTI and DISC. For example, people often assume that Extraverts are just another way of looking at DISC Core I individuals, and that strong Judgers are correlated to DISC Core D's. Although some correlation does exist, we'd like to underscore the fact that your child is an individual, not a statistic. In other words, just because many DISC Core I's are extraverts doesn't mean they all are. We know quite a few Core I's who are Introverts, and Core D's who are Perceivers. Do not make the mistake of misunderstanding your child by making an assumption. If you want to become a student of your student, we urge you to be a *good* student of your student, and study him or her deeply.

Behavioral vs. Cognitive Perceiving and Processing

As promised, we'd like to clarify the difference between Perceiving and Processing on the DISC and the MBTI. To start, because DISC is a behavioral measurement, it's looking at how students engage the material *behaviorally*. Core C's and D's (Type 2 and 3 Learners) perceive new information behaviorally by stepping back and observing it. They are tuned in on the tasks involved, not the people. Core S's and I's (Type 1 and 4 Learners) perceive new information behaviorally through some kind of experience, preferably involving other people.

The MBTI ***Perceiving*** scale has Sensors and Intuitives – the "here and now" sensors, and the "future implication" perceivers. These cognitive (MBTI) differences describe *what* students notice, not how they're noticing it. For example, let's say a Core C / Type 2 Learner is learning about writing applications for Smart Phones. As a Core C / Type 2, he is watching quietly and observing the tasks involved.

That's the how. As for the *what*, if this learner is a Sensor on the MBTI, he is quietly observing the tasks while thinking about all the details he's seeing and hearing. He's focused on the immediate application of the new learning so he can perform tasks well when asked.

However, if this student is an Intuitive, he's quietly observing all the tasks while thinking about the future implications of what he's learning. Perhaps he's thinking of how his new learning can help him write an app that will sell worldwide and make him a lot of money. Or perhaps he's thinking of how he can write an app that will make it easier to send financial aid to orphanages in Haiti.

In other words, this student is *behaving* like a Core C / Type 2 Learner, but the mental activity going on inside his head will vary, depending on whether he's a Sensor or an Intuitive.

Now let's look at how ***Processing*** differs between MBTI and DISC. Let's say a Core S / Type 1 Learner is learning how to make a lamp. As a Core S / Type 1 Learner, this student has first *perceived* the instruction with a "people" perspective. Was the instructor confident or apprehensive? Was he sloppy or neat? Was he personable, or was he more matter-of-fact?

But now it's time to *process* the instruction (that is, finding meaning in it), and a Core S / Type 1 Learner will do that with a hands-off approach while looking for ways to minimize risk. He's watching carefully to ensure he understands the safety issues involved, because he doesn't want to get electrocuted. He also doesn't want to be embarrassed when he has to make his lamp, so he's observing whatever he can to minimize that risk.

That's a little of *how* he's processing. Now let's look into the "what" of his mental processes.

If this student were a Thinker, he would be paying close attention to all the tangible actions expected and the equipment needed. He would also be tuned in to observe where the instructor is concerned about using precision when dealing with the safety concerns. He would also be tracking the steps needed for wiring a lamp in a step-by-step fashion.

However, if this student were a Feeler, he might be thinking about who he would trust to work with when it came time to wire his own lamp. He might also be thinking of ways to secure personalized attention from the instructor during the tricky parts of wiring his own lamp. He might even be watching others, and planning ahead to whom he might want to help in case they just weren't getting it. And, he could also be thinking about how other people might feel after he showed them his completed lamp.

In other words, this student is *behaving* like a Core S / Type 1 Learner, but the mental activity going on inside his head while processing this new learning will vary, depending on whether he's a Thinker or a Feeler.

Know the Spectrums; Use the Information Wisely

If you've identified your student to be strong on either end of any of the four MBTI spectrums, then you have useful information to help "educate your child according to his way." However, if your student is at or near the middle on any or all of the four spectrums, just know that your student is adaptable in those area and is able to adjust to many different learning environments. In those cases, there is no need to make adjustments. The only reason to make adjustments is if your child scores strongly one way or the other on any spectrum.

Taking an MBTI

The really low-cost alternative to identifying one's MBTI Type is to read thoroughly the myriad online descriptions of the four spectrums and the eight tendencies at the ends of those spectrums. You can also get books like *Please Understand Me* by David Keirsey to get a very thorough understanding of the four spectrums. Keirsey's book also contains a 70-question Keirsey Temperament Sorter, which, as mentioned earlier, is a close cousin to the MBTI, as it uses the same four spectrums.

The more you familiarize yourself with the eight functions measured with an MBTI, the better you'll be able to recognize what's going on in your students – and yourself. If you trust your observations and are a devoted student of your students, you will recognize your learner and yourself in the MBTI descriptions.

However, if you desire an accurate picture, you should take an actual MBTI. Just keep in mind that if your student is under the age of 10 they are probably not self-aware enough to answer the questions accurately by themselves. That said, we've administered the Keirsey

Temperament Sorter to kids as young as 8, and by providing synonyms to help explain the words in the assessment, the kids were pretty accurate at identifying their individual styles.

If you want an official MBTI, it must be administered by a certified practitioner. The good news is that thousands of people are certified; The downside is they always want money for these things. If you want instant access to an official MBTI assessment, you can take one online at www.mbtionline.com. The cost (at the time of this writing) is $49.95 for both the online assessment and the accompanying interactive learning experience that goes deeper into the characteristics of your type.

For a much deeper (and more expensive) analysis, the Center for Applications of Psychological Type offers an MBTI and an hour-long phone consultation with a certified MBTI professional for a total cost of $150 (USA pricing at the time of this writing). The MBTI professional will explain your report and answer any questions you have. Their website is www.capt.org.

To be clear, we do not earn anything for mentioning these services, nor, for that matter do we officially recommend them. We simply mention these sites as places you can obtain official MBTI assessments.

No-Cost Alternatives

Many websites offer "free" assessments to determine one's type. As with most things free, keep in mind that you might be "getting what you pay for," because accuracy is often criticized on these free assessments. That said, keep in mind that, from an educational standpoint, it really doesn't matter if your child is near the middle on any given spectrum, and it's in the middle where these free assessments get most of their criticism. Since your concern as a parent is whether your child scores strongly in any of the four areas, the free online assessments will identify that. Then, armed with that knowledge, you can work to create a better learning environment for your student.

Chapter 14
Gender Differences

What do you think when you hear phrases like, "Boys will be boys" or, "You know how girls are"? We're guessing that whatever your answer is, it won't help much in terms of what you can do to help your child learn. Although males have certain attributes that "most" males have, and females have certain attributes that "most" females have, it has been our observation that acting on stereotypes from gender grouping often inhibits growth in a child's natural giftings. Therefore, we don't pay much attention to gender when it comes to understanding students.

Take the statement, "Boys will be boys," and think of when you've heard it. Usually it appears at the end of a description of the child's behavior, his values, or his thinking process, and it's the equivalent of putting one's hands in the air and saying, "There's nothing I can do about it." In practice, it becomes a fatalistic approach. The parent thinks, "A conclusion has been reached, the situation is not likely to change, and we'll just have to cope and settle for whatever we get – because he's a boy."

Let us illustrate why we think using gender classification is not a useful (nor a necessarily healthy) approach to becoming a student of your student. Let's take a 5-year-old who loves playing in the dirt and examining worms, slugs, and every type of bug; who climbs trees with the confidence of a chimpanzee; who runs around making all sorts of noises while doing so, takes risks his parents never would have dreamed of taking at that age, and approaches everyone as if they were all long-lost friends who are just dying to play with him. His imagination runs wild as he comes up with all sorts of ideas and scenarios he wants to explore – making something, experimenting with something else, taking things apart and rebuilding them. He makes up games and wants others to play those games with him. And with all that, getting him to sit down and focus on his school work is like pulling hen's teeth. He's easily distracted and won't sit still to save his life when you're trying to teach him.

Too many people will read the above and say, "Typical five-year old boy." Those people would be assuming too much, because what we just wrote was a description of our daughter at age five.

Here's how we look at the attributes listed above, regardless of whether the child is male or female:

> Loves playing in the dirt, examining worms, slugs, and bugs, climbs trees with confidence: Most likely has a strong *Naturalistic Intelligence*, seeking to understand nature and being very comfortable when doing things outside.
>
> Climbs trees with confidence, likes making things, experimenting on things, taking things apart & rebuilding them, very physically active: Most likely has a strong *Bodily-Kinesthetic Intelligence*, seeking to know the world through physical activity, physical manipulations, and handling objects skillfully.
>
> Highly active, takes risks, strong imagination, strong creativity, wants to interact with practically everybody in almost every situation: Most likely a *Core "I" / Type 4 Learner*.
>
> Highly active, is easily distracted, can't sit still while being taught: Most likely *ADD*, possibly *ADHD*.

Can you see how generalizing the above description as *typically* male or female does little, if anything, to help you as you help your students learn? Yes, statistics show that girls typically do "x," and boys typically do "y," but those statistics are based on how boys and girls *typically* score on the various scales of the factors we've talked about in this book. Your child is unique, so to become a student of your student, you must learn about your student's uniqueness!

True Gender Differences: The Corpus Callosum

Here's something that is definitely true about gender differences. In utero, all babies develop along the lines of a female until the male genetics kick in for boys and things start changing. One change is the testosterone wash of the brain. Seven times during a pregnancy, the male brain receives what amounts to a testosterone wash. As it turns out, the testosterone impacts the corpus callosum, which is the bridge of nerve tissues connecting the left and right sides of the brain. And by impact, we mean "thins it out." The neural networks within each hemisphere remain, but the communication paths *between* the two hemispheres for males ends up to be about 20% less than females.

As Daniel says in his workshops, "That's right guys … we're all brain damaged … and we were born that way."

The upside for most women is that they can process data back and forth faster and in different ways than men can, reaching conclusions much faster. The downside is they can't always tell you HOW they reached those conclusions. Some women bristle at the phrase, "women's intuition," thinking it's a derogatory term, but in truth, it's a compliment. What we call women's intuition is really women processing data much faster than men; but without articulating why or how they reached their conclusions. They just "know." (Men – this is why it's a good idea to trust your wife's gut instinct!)

Another impact of that testosterone wash is how the brain listens. Research from the Kennedy Krieger Institute using brain imaging technology found that women listen with both sides of their brain, whereas men listen with only their left hemisphere. (We'll wait while you think of a few jokes to insert here.)

Of course, with both sides of the brain involved in listening, women do rightfully get to keep the badge of being *able* to listen better, but that might not play out in actual practice. Additionally, we know that plenty of research shows girls outperforming boys in language skills, but we also know that advantage lasts only until junior high / high school years.

Here are some other things we know:

- Boys tend to be diagnosed with dyslexia more than girls.
- Boys tend to be diagnosed with ADHD more than girls.

We could go on with a long list of where boys *tend* to do things differently than girls, and vice versa. But the phrase "tends to" should not – and does not – define an entire population group. As we've been saying, each person is an individual, and there are so many unique factors at play within each individual that making generalized assumptions about a person merely because of gender is unwise.

Another thing to consider is *behaviorism* (the impact of reinforcement regarding behaviors, thoughts, or beliefs). In addition to God-given differences, much of what influences a child's growth is reinforcement. If reinforcement of any behavior or belief is positive, chances are the child will repeat the behavior or adhere more firmly to the belief that received positive reinforcement. The opposite is true if the reinforcement was negative. This is one of the key influences you have as a parent as you train up your child.

Gender and Hemisphericity

You've probably heard it said that men are predominately left-brain dominant (logical), whereas women are considered more right-brained or whole-brained (creative). Please know that these are merely stereotypes. In hemisphericity research conducted at the University of Arkansas and outlined in the book *Brain Dominance and Leadership Style* by Arul Lawrence, 71 percent of people assessed were left-brain dominant, 24 percent were right-brain dominant, and 5 percent were determined to be whole-brain learners. Also in the findings, 66 percent of the people assessed were only slight-to-moderate in their left-brain leanings. This means that just because 66 percent of the entire study group (both male and female) scored as left-brain learners, they weren't exclusively left-brain in their approach to learning. It's just that they relied on left-brain techniques slightly or moderately more than they relied on right-brain techniques.

Later in Lawrence's book is a statement you might find interesting, which we quote directly: "There was no statistical significant association between brain hemisphericity with gender, race, and program of study" (p. 46).

Can you see why we say, "Don't pigeonhole your children using gender stereotypes"? We know many families in which a daughter is left-brained and a son is right-brained. Because your child is unique, the best way to determine your child's hemisphericity to have him complete an assessment, such as the *Hemispheric Mode Indicator*. Then you will know your child's individual hemisphericity and how strong it is, from which you can determine how to adapt your teaching so your student learns better.

DISC & Learning Style Differences

Although gender differences do exist in Learning Styles, we need to point out that the differences are quickly turned into over-generalized statements, and are *not* helpful when talking about individual students. In other words, statements such as "boys are this way, and girls are that way" should not be used. The graph pictured to the right shows the range of scores for males and females in the four different scales (with more than 35,000 people assessed), and each column's shaded area represents how 68% of the gender scored for that given style. As you can see, the amount of *overlap* in the male/female columns for each scale is quite large, and the differences are rather small. Specifically:

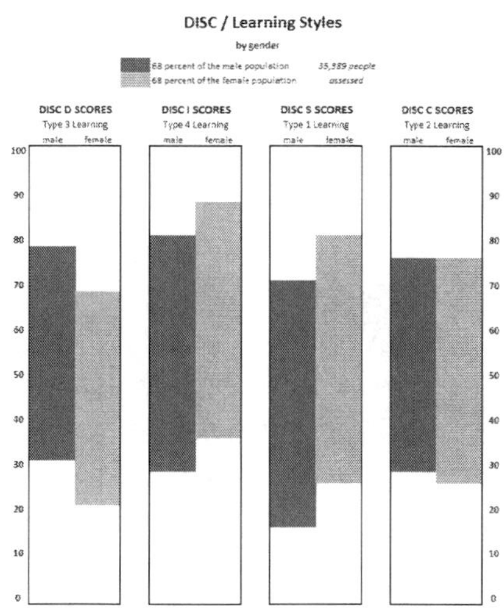

- Males are only 10 % more likely to be a Type 3 Learner/Core D
- Females are only 7.5 % more likely to be a Type 4 Learner/Core I
- Females are only 11 % more likely to be a Type 1 Learner/Core S
- Males are only 1.7 % more likely to be a Type 2 Learner/Core C

Imagine someone saying, "Research has found that right-handed people are 10 percent more likely to select grapes as their favorite fruit than left-handed people. Therefore, since your child is right-handed, he must like grapes." It's not logical. Similarly, "Boys typically do this," and, "Girls typically do that" are statements that "experts" make to show they understand the statistics. Don't let that impress you, because it's really not useful for you. Your child is not a statistic, but rather a unique person created by God with many distinctive facets of individuality. Take the time to know and understand your unique students by "digging deep" to identify their unique learning styles.

Final Thoughts on Gender

As a final thought in this chapter, we are saddened when we encounter families (and churches) that follow narrow perspectives on the roles of males and females. Our daughter absolutely loves science, and as she is finishing seventh grade (at the time of this writing), she scores at the college level in mathematics. Almost her entire life she has expressed interest in being a veterinarian, and should she maintain that interest, her natural, God-given abilities in math, science, and nature will serve her well.

If we had tried pressing our daughter into a "traditional girl" mode (be it conservative or contemporary), she would not be thriving in her God-given talents, and, as we have observed time and again in people all around us, she would likely feel unfulfilled. That said, we readily acknowledge that some girls are naturally drawn to "traditional girl" roles, again, be they conservative or contemporary. The point we've been trying to make throughout this book is to become a student of your students, and train them up in the way they should go (e.g., educate them according to their way), for that is the best way to guide them to the highest degree of fulfillment and a lifetime of joy.

Chapter 15
Special Circumstances

We strongly advocate against labeling children with a disability whenever possible. Children may have conditions that inhibit learning, but when someone's teaching style is different from a student's behavioral / learning style, or when a teacher and student have opposing strengths in their multiple intelligences, too often a "learning disability" is assumed. It's been our observation that once people start looking for a problem, they're going to find one. But even when genuine learning difficulties exist, we recommend that you don't let those conditions become excuses.

To the extent possible, we recommend identifying your student's behavior & learning style, hemisphericity, and his/her innate, natural intelligences, and then working to create situations and learning environments that make it easier for your child to learn.

This is one of the reasons we strongly advocate homeschooling, because students can have their learning curriculum tailored to who they are as individuals. In large classrooms, the teacher, by necessity, must be more of a classroom manager, keeping order and trying to maintain an atmosphere of sanity while trying to teach. When you have 25 to 30 seven-year-olds wiggling in their chairs, it's hard to maintain attention and learning momentum on any given subject. Hats off to the teachers who can manage those classrooms!

That said, in those environments, much of what's going on is classroom management. Kids miss out on a lot, because there is no possible way a classroom teacher can accommodate everyone's learning style. Some learning sticks, and other learning gets missed. It doesn't help that teachers are taught in teacher colleges to "teach to the middle." Students who are slow to learn will have to do their best to keep up, and students who pick up the learning quickly must be patiently bored while waiting for everyone else to "get it."

So, picture this. Let's say your child is a DISC Core I / Type 4 learner who is right-brained and has strong Bodily-Kinesthetic and Verbal-Linguistic intelligences. This child does not want to sit quietly at a desk while perceiving and processing new information! In fact, any child with strong Bodily-Kinesthetic intelligence will not like perceiving and processing information while sitting still. Add the Verbal-Linguistic, right-brained nature, plus the social animal that is the Core I / Type 4 learning style, and it will be like herding cats with this one when it comes to classroom management.

Now consider this: What if this student's instructor is a Core C / Type 2 learner, left-brained, with strong Mathematical-Logical intelligence? Rather than find learning activities that suit our squirrelly student and teach using unfamiliar / uncomfortable methods, such a teacher might find it easier to claim our student is "learning disabled." This happens in institutional schools more than you may realize.

But before we get too far off topic, we suppose we can elaborate more on reasons for homeschooling in another book. For now, let's focus on what truly are "special circumstances." Sometimes learning difficulties occur because of biological issues. Obviously, a couple of chapters in one book cannot cover the entire spectrum of conditions that inhibit learning. Therefore, if you observe that your child continues to have difficulty learning after adjusting for their learning style, hemisphericity, and innate intelligences, we encourage you to research the many resources available to help parents help their students on these many issues. Perhaps someday we will address more than what we write in the next four chapters, but for now, we will address some of the more common issues, and what might be done to accommodate them.

For this book, we will look at four common issues: ADD / ADHD, Asperger's Syndrome, Dysgraphia, and Dyslexia. If these are not issues for you, feel free to skip over these chapters.

Chapter 16
Attention Deficit Disorder (ADD / ADHD)

The problem with ADD and ADHD (the "H" stands for *Hyperactivity*) is that it has become the go-to diagnosis quickly placed on kids who are antsy. In reality, a SPECT brain scan is an actual clinical way to confirm what is called ADD / ADHD, but the use of SPECT scans for diagnosing ADD is *extremely rare*. The diagnosis is almost always made by someone merely saying the student shows signs. And if you have a squirrelly seven-year-old whose natural style is to perceive and process new information through movement, it's easier to slap a label of ADHD on him and feed him drugs than it is to accommodate his unique learning style in a classroom of 25 – 30 kids.

Unfortunately, the practice of labeling kids with this condition (and medicating them for it) is all too common, and it's been going on for a while now. Let's go back to a 2003 *USA Today* article, in which child psychologist Neil Hoffman was quoted as saying, "Schools are quick to recommend solutions before they've fully evaluated the problem." According to Hoffman, "Too often the first reaction to an attention problem is, 'Let's medicate.'" Hoffman was not wrong in his observations. At the time he was quoted, the number of children taking Ritalin had tripled in just five years, and those numbers have not gone down. Other research since that time shows that the number of children being diagnosed with ADD / ADHD goes up more than five percent every year.

It is our opinion that ADD / ADHD treatments are used more for classroom management than they are for improving student learning.

That said, when a child truly does have ADD or ADHD, much better and safer options are available than prescription medications. These include vitamin and amino acid supplements, dietary changes, physical activities, and behavioral plans. We would never claim to be experts, but we know children with ADD / ADHD who have been able to stay focused and learn at a normal pace using one or more of the methods we're about to describe. And, these successes came without dulling the children's personalities to the point of the them becoming drugged-up zombies.

In all of these treatments, your mileage may vary. But, if you're dealing with a potential ADD / ADHD situation, we encourage you to consider these options, investigate them even more for yourself, and customize what you think might work to your specific situation. With medical supervision, of course*.

Vitamin and Amino Acid Supplements

In his book *Healing ADD*, Dr. Daniel Amen identifies seven distinct types of ADD. And, for each type, he recommends a different regimen of supplements. We're not going delve into each of the seven types, because Dr. Amen's website (amenclinics.com) has a free online questionnaire that helps you determine which type of ADD your student may have. Or not. We've seen some people go through all the questions only to learn that ADD / ADHD is not likely. However, if ADD / ADHD is present, the results of your answers to the online questions will tell you which of the seven types is *likely* present – and in some cases it's more than one! And, if you get Amen's *Healing ADD* book, you can learn which type of supplement regimen Dr. Amen recommends. Of course, we are obligated here to say you should always consult some kind of health care professional before providing those supplements to your children*.

We can attest to the fact that we've seen the Amino Acid supplements recommended by Dr. Amen work. We know one squirrelly nine-year-old who became phenomenally more focused when taking an amino acid and vitamin regimen and adding more physical exercise to his daily routine. Assignments that took him four hours to struggle through without supplements were completed in less than one hour with them.

Dietary Changes

The need for dietary changes for people with ADD / ADHD goes beyond the advice of health food advocates. Even the most traditional doctors recommend adjusting the diet for someone with ADD / ADHD. Recommendations include:

- Eat high-quality lean proteins, and consume them sporadically throughout the day
- Restrict carbohydrate intake to low glycemic / high fiber
- Eliminate sugar and food dyes
- Drink plenty of water

One of the most important things to remove from the diet is sugars. When ADD / ADHD children we've worked with have had sugary cereals for breakfast, their morning learning was much like herding cats. We also recommend eliminating sugary snacks (especially the commercially mass-produced snacks that are laden with processed sugar) and giving the kids nuts and berries as snacks instead.

Plenty of information on diet for ADD / ADHD people can be found online, so we encourage you to research this further to get more ideas. Also, Dr. Amen's *Healing ADD* book has a chapter devoted to the subject of diet.

Physical Activity

Between the ADD and the ADHD, physical activity is especially effective for those with ADHD (although students without the hyperactive component will also benefit). Again, the H in ADHD stands for hyperactivity, but perhaps a better way to think of it is kids having too much energy and it's trying to get released! If kids with

ADHD are sitting a lot, they are going to fidget and wiggle, because there's just no other way for that energy to work its way out.

Physical exercise is not only excellent for dissipating excess energy, it also releases neurotransmitters necessary for attention and impulse control. Research documented on WebMD.com has shown that the effect of exercise on ADHD is quite powerful. For example, in studies measuring attention and controlling impulsivity, students with ADHD who exercised scored better than ADHD students who did not exercise, even when no other ADHD treatments were involved.

In practical terms, this means school breaks should not be spent playing games on computers! Playing soccer, tag, Frisbee, or even running laps is a great way to get blood flowing to the brain, and also for releasing those neurotransmitters. After school, it is extremely helpful for ADHD kids to ride bikes, go swimming, go dancing, or ride skateboards. Anything to get them moving. In one study, even a 20-minute walk was found to help ADHD students concentrate better.

Behavioral Plans

Too often, ADD / ADHD students are observed engaging in time-wasting, irrelevant activities. It's very easy to say, "Stop doing that," but nature abhors a vacuum. In other words, "just stopping" is not so easy. What makes it easier is when we offer alternative behaviors, and reward those alternative behaviors when we see them.

We have seen behavioral plans work very well with ADD / ADHD kids. Essentially, you create a grid (or chart) showing the behaviors you want to see, and you grade students on how well they performed each of those behaviors. The grading occurs at several times throughout the day.

Then, at the end of the day, the student receives rewards according to his performance.

You are encouraged to do more research about this idea online, but here is an outline of what we've seen work:

1. Identify the negative behaviors you want gone. Then identify the behaviors you want to see instead.
2. Clearly describe the behaviors you want to see so your student understands them. *Bonus: Have your child assist in creating those behavioral descriptions.*
3. Make a chart that lists the desired behaviors on one axis, and a timeframe on the other.
4. Make your timeframes small. It's best if a student is graded several times throughout the day so he remains aware of what is expected. The idea is "frequent review, quick reward." At the end of the day, if your student acquires "x" number of points, he can get a reward THAT EVENING.

Rewards can (and should) be low cost, such as watching a movie, going to a park, or having friends over. Work with your student to arrive at whatever rewards will be motivating enough for him, but definitely avoid rewarding children with sugar-filled foods or computer games. If you like you can also include larger rewards for multiple days of success, or "x" number of points gathered in a week. This way, even if the student doesn't get enough points for a larger weekly reward, other rewards can have been achieved throughout the week.

Keys to success when using behavior plans include the following:

1. **Use them for a set period of time.** One or two months is a good start. If changes still aren't happening with consistency, you can extend the time frame. Just don't make it eternal.
2. **Be consistent.** If you grade behaviors and give feedback only when you remember, it isn't going to help much. To be successful, consistency is key.
3. **Be encouraging.** Scolding a child isn't very motivating. It's okay to show a little disappointment, but it's better to be encouraging. Also, criticism should be off the table. And be sure to heap praise on every success.

In addition to the book *Healing ADD*, we also would like to suggest the book *Driven to Distraction* by Edward Hallowell, M.D. It provides excellent information and has many case studies that show us there is nothing wrong with having ADD / ADHD. (*Full disclosure: Dr. Hallowell wrote an endorsement of Daniel's first book about removing obstacles to success, but we do not receive compensation by recommending Dr. Hallowell's books*).

Let us also say that because ADD / ADHD conditions can often be treated with supplements, diet, exercise, and behavior plans, we don't refer to ADD / ADHD as a disorder. There is nothing wrong with these children – they are merely *different*, and they are no different from the kids of 50 years ago who were described as being more amped up than others. However, given the way that our culture in the USA has morphed to eating mostly processed foods and kids are sitting in front of computer games instead of throwing Frisbees, flying kites, and riding their bicycles, we've seen an uptick in the ripple effects of those cultural changes, and doctors have labeled it as a disorder.

First Person Account

To provide a first-person perspective, we are providing some quotes from Shilo Urban, a freelance writer from Texas who has had ADD her whole life. On her blog *Organic Authority*, Shilo writes the following about having ADD:

> "ADD is NOT a disorder, despite the name. It is not a learning disability, although it can often accompany them. The brains of people with ADD work very differently than most people's brains do, but that does not mean they are disordered – only different.
>
> "I am blessed with the gift of ADD, and I would not trade my "disorder" for the world. Like most people with ADD, my energy knows no bounds, my enthusiasm is catching, my creativity pays the bills and I am the life of the party.

> "You might think it's odd, but being diagnosed with a "mental disorder" was one of the best things to ever happen to me. Once properly diagnosed, I finally realized that so many of my so-called "failings" had nothing to do with a lack of ability or moral aptitude. People with ADD are like square pegs trying to fit into a world made by round-holers.

To wrap up this chapter, if you have squirrelly learners on your hands, we suggest you first strive to understand everything you can about their God-given learning style, hemisphericity and innate intelligences, and then make adjustments in their learning environments to accommodate their style.

If the squirrelly behavior still exists, we recommend looking into the suggestions made in this chapter (and even others) before turning to the drug option. We realize that prescription drugs may be the only thing that focuses your child's mind enough for him to learn, but we strongly urge you make that the absolute last option, not the first.

* Our stay-out-of-jail obligatory statement: *These statements have not been evaluated by the Food and Drug Administration. This product (i.e., this book containing our opinion) is not intended to diagnose, treat, cure or prevent any disease. Always check with a medical professional before taking or providing any dietary supplements to your children.*

Chapter 17
Asperger's Syndrome

Often considered to be the upper part of the autism spectrum, Asperger's Syndrome gets its name from the Austrian doctor who first described the disorder in 1944 – Hans Asperger. By way of a quick overview, students may have Asperger's Syndrome if they have difficulty communicating (such as looking people in the eye), if they have intense interest in a few areas but totally ignore others, and if they desire their routines in some areas to become almost like a ritual (such as a breakfast routine; what time of day something occurs; what day of the week something occurs).

Many more symptoms exist, so if you think this might be an issue for your learner, do an Internet search to investigate further. Asperger's Syndrome is most often noticed about the same age that communication skills develop, ages 2 – 6, because social skills are extremely difficult for someone with Asperger's to learn.

Just as Shiloh Urban describes having ADD (in the previous chapter) as being a blessing, very cool things can develop in students with Asperger's Syndrome. For example, think about the multiple intelligences. Around the world, almost everyone has two or three strong natural intelligences. But for students with Asperger's, it's common to be *absolutely exceptional* in just one of the intelligences, and score extremely low in most of the others. This is one of the reasons we say don't let the condition of Asperger's become an excuse. Work with your student in his area of strength, and develop that talent!

Oftentimes, people whom we acknowledge as geniuses in certain fields happen to have Asperger's. Consider Albert Einstein. Nobody has a problem tagging him with the "genius" label, but did you know he also had what is now known as Asperger's Syndrome?

As other examples of what we're talking about, consider some of these people who have or were believed to have had Asperger's:

Mathematician and physicist Isaac Newton
Novelist Jane Austen
Poet Emily Dickinson
Composer Ludwig van Beethoven
Inventor Thomas Edison
Actress Daryl Hannah
Singer Susan Boyle
Peanuts cartoonist Charles Schulz

Also, Temple Grandin, a professor of animal science, inventor, and the subject of an award-winning biographical film, has very high-functioning autism, which some professionals equate to having Asperger's Syndrome, since the two are on the same spectrum.

Because no medication exists to treat students with Asperger's Syndrome, the condition requires parents to be supportive, patient, and understanding while working with the student behaviorally. (We would add that it also means becoming a diligent student of your student!) Temple Grandin says that 20 hours per week of interactive games that teach social skills are necessary for steady development of these skills. She also suggests that if you cannot afford a nanny or a professional specialist, to arrange for your child to play such games with some of the older women at your local church.

As previously mentioned, we do not recommend letting Asperger's or any other disorder become an excuse for not learning. Obviously, learning some things will be more uncomfortable for students with Asperger's, and teaching things like executive function (reasoning, planning and organizing, task flexibility, and problem solving) will require much extra time and effort. Your job as a parent will include being flexible and creative as you experiment with what works and what doesn't, and your love (as described in 1 Corinthians 13) and dedication to your student is absolutely necessary.

By the way, when it comes to applying 1 Corinthians 13, we'll need to underscore the word *patience.* In educating children with Asperger's, one axiom is, "Twice as much time, half as much done." However, depending on how severe the condition, that may be true only until you figure out how best to teach to your student's unique style. Conversely, teaching may actually take longer, too.

One suggestion that's true with all Asperger students is to maintain consistency wherever possible. Unplanned and sudden changes can cause confusion, frustration, and also levels of discomfort. That said, it's also vital to inform an Asperger's student that "life happens." When schedule changes must occur, use them as an opportunity to discuss – and practice – appropriate coping attitudes and behaviors. And be sure to heap praise on those healthy attitudes and behaviors when they are displayed. We've seen overprotective parents inhibit their child's growth by not helping their child learn coping skills. This only reinforces excuses and dependency, which will not serve the child well after entering the world of work.

Students with Asperger's often have difficulty distinguishing between essential and non-essential information. Accordingly, they also have difficulty reading between the lines, and can have a difficult time attaching new learning to past learning to develop what is commonly referred to as "common sense." Therefore, as we mentioned, the "Twice the time, half as much done" mindset will be the case more often than not, and sometimes it will be "Four times the time, one fourth as much done."

Perhaps one of the easiest ways to think about someone with Asperger's is to consider him to be an ultimate left-brained, Core C / Type 2 learner. And we mean Core C / Type 2 Learner *to the extreme.* Emotions? Don't expect much. Factual? Expect a lot. Read as much as you can find about DISC Core C behavior / Type 2 Learners. Magnify those attributes and you pretty much have someone with Asperger's. The main difference will be that children with Asperger's do not incorporate the typical Core C / Type 2 strengths of diplomacy and courteousness. Those are part of the social skills that are difficult to learn. Instead of tact you're likely to encounter uninhibited blunt truth, but you can work with that over time. Basically, if you maintain communications as if you were talking with a pure Core C / Type 2 Learner, you'll be on the right track.

With that, let us emphasize the need to be just as courteous and kind when talking to someone with Asperger's as you are when you're talking with anyone else, even when you're not getting any indication that they're tracking you. People with Asperger's tend to display emotional flatness, and many people tend to think they're being rude when that's not the case at all. Here is where the phrase, "Still waters runs deep," comes back into play. Author John Elder Robison, in his book, *Be Different: Adventures of a Free-Range Aspergian*, describes many scenes in which he would inadvertently offend people simply because he hadn't learned how to be socially interactive. In Robison's Aspergian mind, facial expressions were not considered part of communication, they were just faces. And so, when talking with a student with Asperger's, don't expect body language to be a factor in their communication equation. Talk with them as you would with any Core C and keep the conversation going.

With that, to help students with Asperger's get along better with others, you'll want to spend extra time helping them learn about reading facial expressions. Several such charts are available online, and your time spent in this effort is profoundly helpful for your student. Show them a human facial expression and explain what the expression conveys. Start with the six basic emotions of happy, angry, sad, surprised, fearful, and disgusted. Work with your student so he can match the appropriate term to the correct facial expression, then build on that by helping them understand what those emotions mean – and when someone might experience them. Do this over and over and over, and continue doing it even when they're explaining all the emotions correctly and why people might experience them. And be sure to provide your students with heaps of praise and/or rewards.

Although the six basic emotions is a good place to start, you don't want to stop there. Research has revealed that at least 21 facial expressions are practically universal in western society. In a March,

2014 press release from Ohio State University, Dr. Aleix Martinez, a cognitive science researcher at the University said:

> We've gone beyond facial expressions for simple emotions like 'happy' or 'sad.' We found a strong consistency in how people move their facial muscles to express 21 categories of emotions. 'That is simply stunning. That tells us that these 21 emotions are expressed in the same way by nearly everyone, at least in our culture.'

The photographs from Martinez's research can be found online by searching for, "21 facial expressions." These would be an excellent resource for working with your student on this learning.

Along these same lines, it's also important to help Asperger's students learn to display appropriate, acceptable body language themselves. The Behavior Modification Plans described in the previous chapter on ADD/ADHD may prove beneficial in this effort.

By the way, know that people with Asperger's can "rabbit trail" fairly easily with their learning. In *Be Different*, Robison describes being told to read a chapter in a book and then complete an assignment on it. As Robison started reading, he "got into it" and read the entire book! Then, because the subject matter piqued his curiosity, he began another book on the subject, and forgot his original assignment. Robison says this happened a lot. He learned much along the way, but because he neglected his assignments, he received poor grades.

Be on the lookout for this kind of behavior, and "reel in" your student if necessary. However, if you're a homeschooling parent, these are perfect opportunities to let your student explore and learn.

On the other side of that coin, sometimes students with Asperger's don't see a reason to learn something, and when that happens they often resist learning it. A suggestion we've seen work well is tying the subject matter to a student's long-term aspirations, which then activates their internal motivation to learn.

For instance, if an Asperger's student wants to build game consoles for his future profession yet doesn't see a need for learning geometry or art, inform him that eventually he'll have to work with other designers, because nobody designs a game console and takes it to market all by himself. Therefore, he'll need to understand geometric and artistic principles in order to communicate effectively about design dimensions when working with other designers in the future.

Granted, teaching children with Asperger's can test your patience. You may see minimal improvement for a long time and think nothing is working, but then "BAM" – something seems to click inside of your student and suddenly you have learning. Therefore, never make excuses, and don't allow any, either. Just exercise patience.

The suggestions offered in this chapter are merely a few in the vast amount of things you can do to help an Asperger's student learn and function better. If you suspect your young child may have Asperger's, you will definitely want to read up and become as educated as possible, as well as seek professional assistance. But, as always, our foundational recommendation is do not let the condition become an excuse for not learning.

John Robison underscores this same philosophy in *Be Different*. In a section he calls, "The Danger of Diagnosis," Robison writes:

> Some people read what's associated with a label and make it self-fulfilling. They let go and become the worst of what they read. That negative outcome can be reinforced by teachers and parents who say or think, "He has a diagnosis of autism. We can't expect too much of him."

Robison gets it. He knows that people tend to look for excuses so they don't have to press forward and gain skills. So again, never make excuses, and don't allow any, either.

Interestingly, Robison also echoes our philosophy to stay focused on a student as an individual, not as part of a statistical norm. He says, "It does not matter what sixty-six percent of people do in any particular situation. All that matters is what you do."

Chapter 18
Dysgraphia

Picture yourself in the 1950's and your child's teachers tell you that you son is borderline mentally retarded and definitely emotionally disturbed. "Back in the day," such children were removed from schools, because schools said they didn't have the resources to handle special education needs like that.

The student described above as mentally retarded and emotionally disturbed was Pete Wright, now co-owner of the special education website, wrightslaw.com. Thankfully, through the help of a family friend who was doing research for a graduate paper at the time, Wright was diagnosed with two different disorders; what we now know as dysgraphia and dyslexia.

In short, *dyslexia* is a condition that interferes with the brain's ability to read (we'll look at dyslexia in the next chapter). In this chapter we're looking at ***dysgraphia***, a condition that interferes with a person's ability to write.

In dysgraphia, the parts of the brain that process thoughts, images, and words don't connect well with the motor-function part of the brain that tells the hand how to scribe those thoughts, images, and words into letters on a page. In other words, the sequence of motor movements required to write numbers and letters is not communicating well with the rest of the brain.

Undiagnosed, children with dysgraphia are often viewed as lazy, not caring, or, like Pete Wright, even "dumb" and emotionally disturbed. The truth is that kids with dysgraphia are often VERY smart. So, when you're super smart but you can't write, being labeled as lazy or dumb and getting laughed at by your peers is often emotionally traumatic and plays havoc with your self-esteem.

One of the problems here is that dysgraphia is not as well-known as ADD/ADHD, Asperger's, or dyslexia, so it often goes undiagnosed. Unfortunately, we've seen children with undiagnosed dysgraphia cry for hours while trying to write assignments – not only for the frustration of not being able to do an assignment, but because the act of writing actually causes physical pain for someone with this condition.

Consider the following, submitted to us by a teenager who was diagnosed with dysgraphia:

> I have a train of thought, but I can't write it down. I think in pictures, but I can't translate it well. When I try to write, the tips of my fingers start to ache, and then the joints of my hand start to hurt. I have to stop and flex my hand quite a bit. Then my arm starts to hurt. I have to take breaks because it hurts to write. And every time I write it hurts my head. If I write for a long time, my head hurts *a lot*. My definition of dysgraphia is when your brain doesn't want to translate pictures into letters.

Interestingly, when this student learned about cursive, things got a little bit easier for her, but not much. This student also tells us, "Cursive is a mix between drawing and writing. It hurts less. It doesn't require as much concentration, and I don't have to take as many breaks. Typing also helps. It's weird. It's moving my fingers, but it doesn't hurt like holding and moving a pencil."

If you see any of the following symptoms in your child, he or she *may* have dysgraphia:

- Feeling pain while writing
- Difficulty translating ideas into written words
- Poor handwriting
- Poor word and/or margin spacing
- Excessive erasing
- Cramped fingers and/or odd arm positioning

If any of these are observed, we recommend doing more research online to compare your child's situation to a longer list of possible symptoms. Of course, you should also get input from a healthcare professional*.

As far as treating dysgraphia, one of the best approaches is getting both sides of the brain talking more with each other. You can do this through *cross lateral exercises*. An example of one such exercise is to have your student lift one knee and tap the top of his thigh with the opposing hand, then immediately lift the other knee and tap that knee with the opposite hand, all while walking across the room.

Any cross lateral exercises will help. For more ideas, do an Internet search using the term "cross lateral exercises" and you'll find several worthwhile sites and even videos with these types of brain-building activities.

Additionally, we suggest helping your child by "taking dictation." In other words, they talk, you type. This will get them through assignments to prove they've acquired the requisite knowledge, just don't do their work for them. You're merely the scribe, and nothing else. As the child gets older you can get a computer program that teaches kids how to type. Many such programs now have interactive games that make learning to type more fun.

At the same time, you still want to keep giving your child short, daily writing assignments – they still need that skill! And, when you can wean them onto cursive, by all means do that, as most students with dysgraphia report that writing in cursive is easier than printing letters to make words.

*Our stay-out-of-jail obligatory statement: *These statements have not been evaluated by the Food and Drug Administration. This product (i.e., this book containing our opinion) is not intended to diagnose, treat, cure or prevent any disease. Always check with a medical professional before taking or providing any dietary supplements to your children.*

Chapter 19
Dyslexia

The last condition we'll address in this section on special circumstances is ***dyslexia***, which involves a difficulty in reading text or interpreting words and letters. Unfortunately, between 10 - 15% of the population has dyslexia at some level, and most people with mild forms of dyslexia go undiagnosed.

Federal law mandates that if any child attending a government (public) school is diagnosed with dyslexia, then an Individualized Education Program (IEP) must be created for that student – meaning the child is considered disabled.

But we don't think a child with dyslexia has to be labeled disabled, and neither does Yvonna Graham.

In her book, *Dyslexia Tool Kit for Tutors and Parents* (co-authored with her daughter, Alta), Graham says that dyslexia is a *difference*, not a disability. And we agree. In this ground-breaking book, the Grahams explain, "Dyslexics use right brain skills more heavily than non-dyslexics. They see forests, not trees. They see patterns, not lines. They see context, not text."

And the Grahams should know. While in kindergarten, Alta had not mastered the alphabet, or numbers, or even tying her shoes. Once in first grade, her instructor and school administrators pronounced Alta to be "uneducatable." The stigmas they placed on the girl turned her from being full of life to being terrified and "clingy." Thankfully, Yvonna and her husband removed Alta from the government school system and set out to educate their daughter themselves.

And educate her they did. Alta now holds a Doctorate in Music and is a professor at a college in Colorado. She reads three times faster than her mother, and with better comprehension.

The following are excerpts from Alta Graham's preface to their book:

> I think the saddest word in the history of dyslexic education is "despite." In many dyslexic people, "despite" seems to define who they are in their own minds: "If I work harder than anyone else, maybe I can get a college degree *despite* being dyslexic.... I passed Algebra II *despite* being a dyslexic."
>
> These statements are expressions of great personal triumph, of overcoming adversity, but they are also acceptances of limitation, a way of saying, 'I am dyslexic first, and anything else is secondary to that.'
>
> I am a dyslexic, but because my parents were willing to try technique after technique with tremendous patience, and above all were willing to let me be who I actually was, instead of who the public school authorities told them I was, I didn't grow up covered in 'despite.' '*Because*' replace it, and works much better. *Because* phonics are useless to me, I speed read far faster than my non-dyslexic peers.... *Because*, as a dyslexic, left and right are much the same to me, I can 'flip' shapes and equations in my mind, and thus see patterns in math that my non-dyslexic peers miss.

We love this preface by Dr. Graham. It provides a perfect example of parents becoming students of their student, and just look at the amazing results. The "experts" in education said Alta was *uneducatable*, but her parents proved them wrong. They chose to study their daughter's learning abilities, then taught her using the ways that worked for her.

Although that's a great testimony to the power of becoming a student of your students, the issue in this chapter is still dyslexia, so let's get back to that.

By now you may have realized that Alta's dyslexia was not a typical dyslexia. Yvonna first tried teaching with phonics, but phonics was not working, so Yvonna embarked on a long quest of study with much trial and error, looking for ways to help her daughter read. In the Grahams' book you will find many different methods, but never do they say "*this* is the method – use this." Instead they recommend trying phonics first, because it's the easiest method for teaching. Then, if phonics is not working, they say to consider the book to be a tool box with a wide variety of options.

We're going to echo that sentiment. If your child has dyslexia, there's no reason to settle for "despite." Instead, we recommend getting a copy of *Dyslexia Tool Kit for Tutors & Parents* and trying some of the alternative methods. If the method you chose gets results, great. If not, try another. The book contains two dozen different methods for helping students with dyslexia learn how to read. We don't earn so much as a cent for recommending their book; we just believe it is the biggest possible bang for your buck as you endeavor to teach your dyslexic student how to read.

We don't want to sound like the Grahams' publicists, but when mainstream education says to keep pounding phonics and phonics is not working … well … you know the definition of insanity, right?

With permission from the Grahams, here is one of the tools from their Tool Kit (edited for space):

> **Tool #3: Tracking**.
>
> Before entertainment overload, adults reading while children looked at the book was a common way to pass the evening. It's now uncommon to have reading at home. However, readers with dyslexia need to see and hear the words simultaneously and in context – in a meaningful story or sentence – to remember them!

How to do it: Tell the student, *"I am going to read aloud while you read silently. We will read this sentence.* (Point to the first word.) *The words I say will go into your ears and your eyes at the same time. They will get hooked together in your brain. If you lose the place put your hand up and I will point to where we are. You can stop me as many times as you need. When you stop me it tells me you are really paying attention."*

Then start slowly. Repeat the sentence until the student can keep up visually. Gradually increase speed. Use a finger or pointer to help the student track at first, then back off only to indicate a new line, then eventually only indicate paragraphs. Do NOT block the text below what you are reading because the student needs to be able to "preview" what is ahead using peripheral vision. (*The authors then explain more of the reasons why it is vital to NOT block words on the page*.)

This process can happen in one session for some students, but could take several weeks for others. Always go at the student's pace. Enter the student's time; don't make the student enter "frustrated adult time."

In their book, the Grahams explain much more about how to use the Tracking technique. Plus they offer 23 other techniques about how to enhance learning for dyslexic students.

Since *Dyslexia Tool Kit for Tutors & Parents* costs less than one trip to a reading specialist, it's probably worth your investment. You can learn more about Yvonna Graham's tutoring model for students with dyslexia at *mumblingmarmot.com*, and more about the Grahams' book at *dyslexiakit.net*.

Chapter 20
A Thought on "Official Diagnosis"

If your child is in a government school, a private school, or is planning on entering college, getting an *official* diagnosis of a "learning disability" may be necessary. We often advocate against getting the official diagnosis, because then it becomes easier for kids to "become the diagnosis," using it as an excuse for not learning. However, in the situations listed above, an official diagnosis may be necessary. Here are some examples of why:

Students with dysgraphia have a *horrific* time taking notes, and a certified disability allows them to use audio or video recorders to capture information from lectures. Some instructors and professors at institutional schools are sticklers for "the old tried and true," and may insist that students take hand-written notes. A certified diagnosis tells those instructors to stick it in their ear, and allows students to learn in ways that work for them.

ADD / ADHD students often do better when working at standing desks. Institutional schools may not want to accommodate that. An official diagnosis can tell the school they have to provide that standing desk.

You get the idea.

We remain strong in our belief that a learning "disability" is really just a difference in how someone learns, and neither parents nor students should use an official diagnosis as an excuse for not learning. Therefore, if you must get an official diagnosis, use it only to enable a student to learn in the ways that work for him.

Chapter 21
Make Learning Safe

Part of our job as parents is to keep our children safe, and that certainly applies when we're helping them learn. Learning involves risk. If even the simplest question is answered incorrectly, children can feel devastated, fearful that they have disappointed you and that you will think of them as "less than."

In learning environments, fear stops people from acquiring the knowledge, skills, and attitudes needed to be successful. Therefore, parents should work to minimize unhealthy fears and foster atmospheres of acceptance and growth, instead.

Consider Mike, a young, active boy. Nothing he did seemed good enough for his father. It didn't matter what Mike did, he was criticized while doing it, and mocked afterwards. For example, when Mike turned six, his mother wanted Mike involved in sports, so she enrolled him in a soccer league. Not only did Mike's father never work with him in learning any rules or techniques for how to play, he openly mocked and laughed at Mike at the games. The rest of the team's parents grew tired of hearing "*Mike! Mike!! – Oh come on!*" when Mike wasn't doing something right on the field. Then, after the games, the father would make fun of Mike's mistakes, calling him a doofus for being so inept.

Mike started out as an outgoing child who wanted to try everything, but by the time he hit nine years old, he was declining invitations to try new things. You could see it on his face. His face would light up when he was asked if he wanted to join others in doing something, but if he thought a possibility existed that he might not do well at it, he would almost immediately shake his head and say, "No, thanks." Because of the ongoing criticism he received from his father, Mike's love for learning many new activities died.

Maybe you've seen parents like this. Maybe you *are* a parent like this. And while the type of criticism in the above story was about Mike's physical abilities, we've also seen students shut down inside because they were being criticized about their mental abilities.

Fears can come from many places and be demoralizing, so we strongly suggest that parents work to locate the sources of fear and minimize their impact. This helps to maximize learning, thus giving your child a greater sense of fulfillment.

Sources of Fear

When we look at the sources of fear, we must start with where fear originated: In the book of Genesis, chapter three. In that chapter, Adam and Eve were two perfect people living in a perfect environment and having a perfect relationship with a perfect God. One day they made a huge mistake, and when God went to meet with them, they hid because they were afraid.

There it is. The first mention of fear. Adam and Eve knew they had lost something precious. They knew they had made a mistake. They were afraid of their creator's criticism, his rejection, and their loss of standing in the Garden. In all of that, they were probably afraid of being labeled as failures, too.

Those fears are still here. Think about it. As children, we didn't want our parents (our creators) to criticize or reject us. We didn't want to be seen as failures, and we didn't want to lose whatever safety we might have had in our family structure. Criticism and rejection hurt!

Have you ever had a child bring you something that they made, and start explaining all of what's wrong with it before showing it to you? This is a self-protection technique that minimizes any pain they will feel if imperfections in their work are noticed by you or someone else. It's like saying, "I already know what's wrong with it. I'm identifying the flaws to prove I already know my work is bad. This way, if or when you criticize my work, it won't hurt as much."

They'll never actually say that, and they probably aren't even aware they're using a self-protection technique, but that's the mindset of someone who does that (even if that someone is an adult).

We often see this self-protective "pre-emptive explanation" coming from children whose parents frequently criticize them. It also shows itself in kids who are in classroom environments, for, as the axiom goes, children can be cruel in their honesty. But if children are criticized too much, like in the story about Mike, many kids will shut down and just stop trying.

Bob Amburn is a retired elementary school principal. After 37 years in the public school system, Bob was apprehensive when he learned his grandchildren were being homeschooled. However, over time, he became a believer when he saw that homeschooling provides a much more personalized and emotionally safe environment for learning. He was especially amazed at seeing his 7- and 10-year-old grandkids doing art projects in a public setting. "Very few kids that age at my school would do that," Bob told us. "They would be too afraid of being laughed at or being called a failure by their peers if they didn't do things perfectly."

Even at that young age, too many kids are afraid of learning new things, simply because they have already been criticized so much.

And while we know that criticism runs rampant in institutional school settings, we also know that siblings can be a source of criticism, as well. For example, when 9-year old Julie decided she wanted to bake a cake from scratch and forgot to add the baking powder, the cake didn't rise much. Not only was it flat, it was rather hard. When her parents weren't around, Julie's brothers teased her about the likelihood of them breaking their teeth should they risk taking a bite of her "kitchen disaster." With their harsh words, Julie's spirit was crushed, and she didn't want to bake much after that.

You might say Julie needed to learn to deal with a cruel world, but we say people learn at their own pace. And yes, sometimes all it takes is one such flurry of criticism to squelch a child's desire to learn.

When mistakes are made (and everybody makes them), we recommend adopting the mindset that the mistake is done – it's over – it's past tense. No possibility exists to go back and change what happened. Instead, what can happen—and should happen—is a criticism-free dialog on what was learned and what could be done differently in the future. No long-term productivity comes from dwelling on mistakes. A better alternative is to shift our focus.

Look Three Places

When your children make mistakes or something doesn't go well, consider teaching them to "look three places" afterwards.

Look up, Look down, and Look ahead

To *look up* means to identify what went well. To *look down* means to identify what didn't go so well. And to *look ahead* means to figure out how something could be done differently in the future.

By teaching your children this process, you are equipping them with a tool that reduces the likelihood of them becoming victims, and increases their ability to get past life's inevitable obstacles.

Fear of Loss

Almost all fears are rooted in a fear of loss. Adam and Eve were afraid that they had lost God's acceptance (fear of rejection), that they had lost God's approval (fear of criticism), and that they had lost the only thing they had ever known: A successful life in the Garden (fear of failure). Allow us to quickly address these fears in light of a learning environment.

Fear of Rejection

Rejection can happen in a mere moment. Consider the somewhat introverted 14-year old boy who approached his father and said, "Dad, I think I'd like to be a lawyer." His father's immediate response was, "You don't want to be a lawyer. They have to do a lot of things you wouldn't want to do."

In an instant the boy's dreams crumbled. He had been thinking about becoming a lawyer for a long time. He'd watched lawyers on television, and they were his main focus when he came across them in books. He'd even read up about law school entry requirements, and was excited about the idea. But in the span of that short, 10-second conversation, his father, in essence, had said, "I don't believe in you. Your interests are not worth pursuing."

It wasn't the only time his father had ignored the teen's dreams, but that day was a turning point in the boy's life. Believing that his father didn't care about his future, the boy started hanging out with the wrong crowd at school. In a few months he was experimenting with drugs, and by the time he was 17 he was dealing those drugs.

Please don't think we're saying that the father's 10-second conversation was what turned the boy down the difficult road he chose. What we are saying is that when children fear rejection, they stop trying. And although a one-time rejection *can* be a turning point in a child's life, more often than not the fear of rejection grows out of a long history of criticism.

Fear of Criticism

The stories of Mike and Julie in the first part of this chapter are examples of what can happen when children are criticized. Mike endured ongoing criticism before he finally started shutting down, and for Julie it was one embarrassing, emotionally debilitating day in her life, with nobody knowing how to walk her through *Look up, Look down, and Look ahead.*

As we said, everyone makes mistakes. In fact, according to a quote often attributed to President Theodore Roosevelt, "The man who makes no mistakes does not usually make anything." The key, as Daniel points out in his book, *Removing Obstacles to Success*, is to make only *new* mistakes. Making the same mistakes over and over indicates a lack of learning. But, when a person receives enough criticism for his mistakes, eventually he stops trying to make anything.

Our recommendation is to teach your students to face each mistake and then Look up, Look down, and Look ahead.

Fear of Failure

One of the biggest lies in the world is that people are failures. Failure has to do with circumstances—*not people.* Communicating that a child is a failure kills hope. A child's sense of hope may not die immediately, but if he is repeatedly told he is a failure, his belief that he can have future success fades away.

It's important for parents to communicate a failure as a mistake, and not let a failed attempt define the person who made the mistake. If nothing else, recall the story about Thomas Edison, who was asked how he felt after failing more than 10,000 times to make a working light bulb. Edison's response was that he did not fail 10,000 times, but that he merely found 10,000 ways that would not work.

Although he probably didn't use our phase, Edison was well-practiced in the philosophy of Look up, Look down, and Look ahead.

A Word about Anger

Anger can stop learning in its tracks. As a parent, you "control the weather" in your home. If your child does something wrong and you get—and stay—upset for the entire day, what purpose does it serve?

Without pulling any punches, we say continuing all day with anger is a selfish behavior for the parent, and it only harms the child. The child ends up feeling criticized, rejected, and even abandoned.

We believe it is okay to get angry, but the Bible is pretty clear about how to deal with it: "In your anger, do not sin." Children don't feel safe in an atmosphere filled with anger. We like the "Jekyll/Hyde" approach: If you get angry, be angry and be done with it. Then switch back to the normal you. The child will know he's done wrong, and you can move on with life. It's amazing how effective that can be.

If you tend to get angry a lot, *The Anger Workbook* by Les Carter and Frank Minrith is a useful resource.

Chapter 22
Tying It All Together

In teacher colleges, one of the first things teachers are supposed to learn is that there are three areas in which learning occurs. Those areas are:

- Skills – Things we have to do
- Knowledge – Things we must know to do the skills
- Attitudes – Things we must be concerned about

At least they're supposed to learn that. And then they are supposed to take learning objectives and break them down into digestible chunks of learning, and transfer that learning piece-by-piece in the classroom so our children can function as productive members of our society.

But institutional schools cannot possibly accommodate all the different nuances that enable a student to learn best, so they must, by necessity, look at statistics and teach to the middle portion of their students.

Students who learn quickly are forced to wait patiently while everyone else catches up. Slower students – whom we define as students who learn differently from how the class is being taught – are expected to, "Pick up enough to get by," in the time allotted.

But learning is more than just the acquisition of knowledge, skills, and attitudes. We believe learning involves discovering who God made us to be. As parents, we are in the unique position to observe our students (our children) in all aspects of life. Then, as we notice their tendencies, we can help our students grow via healthy methods into their area of calling. This is the shoe leather part of Proverbs 22:6. This is what we are supposed to do in response to that verse.

We cannot expect institutional schools to perform this task for us. In many cases, people working in the education system do not even know their own children well, so how can we expect them to know ours enough to guide our children into their areas of calling?

This book has been designed as a guide to help you understand the uniqueness of your students. As you apply what you learn, you can help them blossom into vibrant human beings and help them discover God's call on their lives.

And so, let's recap the core of what we've covered, and tie some things together so you can be better equipped to train up your child in the way he should go.

DISC & Learning Styles

If you do nothing else suggested in this book, determine your student's DISC / Learning Style. It will help you in choosing / adapting curriculum and delivering your lessons so your children are engaged. The following story shows how powerful it can be to know your child's style:

> A mother is excited to start homeschooling her five-year old daughter, and she buys a kindergarten math curriculum similar to what she used – and loved – in elementary school. She's eager to see her daughter sail through math as easily as she did, but quickly learns that isn't going to happen. Every day is wrought with frustration and tears from both the daughter and the mother. This little girl hates math! She is repulsed by the worksheets and doesn't want to do them. By mid-year, the mother is at a loss for how to proceed.
>
> One day the mother hears about learning styles. She discovers she scores very strongly in both DISC types S and C (Type 1 and 2 learning styles). She also determines that her daughter is a very strong DISC Core I (Type 4 learner) – a style that does not like worksheets, but rather some kind of hands-on learning.

> The mother then buys the *Right Start* math curriculum, which is very much hands-on and interactive. The turnaround in her daughter is amazing. In fact as the girl finishes sixth grade, whenever someone asks about her favorite subject, she always answers, "Math."

In addition to selecting appropriate curriculum, you can use what you know about your student's learning preference to adapt the curriculum you have.

For example, Jeralynne uses the KONOS curriculum in our homeschooling environment. The curriculum offers a variety of activities to help students engage the material, and by knowing the learning styles of each student, Jeralynne selects activities that she knows will appeal to the children's learning preferences. She also uses her knowledge of each child's learning style to set up optimal learning environments. The Core C / Type 2 learner gets to sit by himself and work quietly. The Core I / Type 4 learner gets to engage with the Core S / Type 1 learner and talk about what they're learning.

Of course, there are always things that get taught with everyone present, but if a student is having a difficult time grasping something, she sets up a learning environment that will help bring success.

Hemisphericity

If knowing your student's DISC / Learning Style is helpful, knowing the student's hemisphericity doubles the amount of helpfulness. Your awareness of which side of the brain your child prefers helps you tailor your teaching so that your student grasps the information more quickly, and in ways that help him apply it more readily.

Knowing the student's dominant hemisphere can also help you figure out why your student may be struggling. Jody and her 15-year old daughter Sasha were fairly similar in their DISC / Learning Style profiles, and also very close in their MBTI scores. But Jody was regularly confused – and frustrated – with several things. Sasha loved to write, but she could not remember grammar rules. She did great on essay questions, but struggled with multiple choice. Nothing was making sense to Jody. Their DISC and MBTI scores were so close, why the differences and struggles in these areas?

Jody's answer came when she discovered Sasha was extremely right-brained, which was very different from Jody's very whole-brained wiring. After Jody learned this, she knew how to adapt so that Sasha would catch on more quickly. By the way, this knowledge improved their relationship, too.

Multiple Intelligences

As previously mentioned, in the world of education, we can divide learning into three teachable areas: knowledge, skills, and attitudes. In his *Train-the-Trainer* workshops, Daniel refers to these as, "Head, Hands, and Heart." He also says it's important to know that our *Head* and *Heart* always drive what we do with our *Hands*.

In the educational realm, we use specific assessments to identify preferences in these three areas:

- Head – The Hemispheric Mode Indicator and MBTI
- Hands – DISC and Learning Styles assessments
- Heart – Multiple Intelligences

In light of Proverbs 22:6, a student's preferences in the Multiple Intelligences give us insights into which direction God might be calling him. For example, our daughter scores strongly in Bodily-Kinesthetic and Naturalistic Intelligences. Considering she has always wanted to be a veterinarian, this make sense.

Robert scores strongly in Interpersonal, and interestingly, he wants to be a marriage/family therapist. And Barb scores strongly in Visual-Spatial, Bodily-Kinesthetic, and Interpersonal. With that, it's not surprising that she's going to school to be a hair stylist.

Multiple Intelligences can also help us align learning with our learners' motivations. One woman we know had a son in public school that was being held back in third grade for the *third year in a row*. His mother said, "NO!" She did not want her son to be three years older and one foot taller than everyone else in his class. She knew he didn't grasp math and language well, but she knew he was an absolute *genius* musically. She pulled him out of school and taught him at home, using music in every way she could. They would write songs about historic events. They'd set poetry to music. They used musical scales as the foundation for teaching math. Just about everything revolved around music, and he finished the rest of his education that way.

The Multiple Intelligences assessment is also useful for knowing where we should tread lightly. Lora scores low on Visual-Spatial, so her mother knows not to press her too much in doing art projects. Eric scores low on Bodily-Kinesthetic, so his mother declined getting him involved in team sports, opting instead that he get exercise by going for walks in the park, because he scores well in Naturalistic.

Cognitive Measures (MBTI)

The MBTI measures things we cannot see: What the brain is likely focusing on in the perceiving, processing, and decision-making processes. Like the Hemispheric Mode Indicator and the Multiple Intelligences, the MBTI is useful for determining what's driving someone's DISC / Learning Style. The following story will help clarify.

Dave was a 16-year-old who tested very strongly as a DISC S/I, with a very low D/C score. His parents validated that, saying Dave loved people, and that he wasn't too keen on following rules or getting things done quickly. He also tested very strongly as right-brained, and his two highest Multiple Intelligences scores were *Interpersonal* and *Intrapersonal*. This indicated Dave was creative, and had a natural proclivity to understand others, as well as himself.

What Dave's parents couldn't figure out was why Dave was so hesitant to commit to being anywhere, and why, when he went places, he wanted to leave early. This didn't seem like typical behavior for someone scoring strongly in both S and I. Dave's parents also thought it odd that he would challenge people's conclusions, knowing strong S-styles are not fond of confrontation. These behaviors kept Dave's parents guessing as to the best way to present information to him. They were doing okay, but they thought they could be doing better.

After Dave completed an MBTI assessment, Dave's parents had their answers. Dave's scores were extreme in all four of the MBTI spectrums, and because cognitive and attitudinal preferences drive behaviors, his MBTI scores were the source of Dave's seemingly quirky behavior.

Dave scored as an extreme Introvert and an extreme Perceiver. This explained why he would not commit to being anywhere, and why he left parties and other functions early. Perceivers like keeping their options open, and Introverts get drained being around people. Dave's scores were extreme, so these preferences really affected him.

Additionally Dave scored extremely high on Intuitive and Thinker. This meant forward thinking, and very objective in that thinking. Combined with his strong Perceiver score, this helped explain why Dave confronted people whenever they made a declarative statement; he was uncomfortable whenever decisions were made. It was never an in-your-face confrontation, it was merely a soft, persistent questioning, such as, "Are you sure? Couldn't it be different?" Dave's super strong Perceiver score indicated he did not like definitive conclusions.

With a full profile of Dave's Head, Heart, and Hands preferences, his parents had a much better picture for how to help Dave learn:

1. <u>Give him options</u>. Dave would choose an activity that suited him best at the moment.

2. <u>Create small-group situations</u>, and let Dave participate to the depth he wants. His love for people gave him a desire to interact, but his *Introvert* and *Perceiver* scores meant he didn't care for forced participation.

3. <u>Play lots of games</u>. Dave liked to have fun. Games that were structured around his learning objectives appealed to his CORE I and right-brained attributes.

4. <u>Present a balance of task and people</u>, and don't' stay too long on either one. As a strong *Thinker* and strong DISC S, Dave preferred a balanced blend of people- and task-activities.

The Big Picture

As you can see, knowing our student's learning preferences in the areas of Head, Heart, and Hands gives us a big picture view of how to connect our children with the world around them.

To repeat what we said earlier, if you could do only one, discover your student's DISC / Learning Style. Obviously, the more you know about your student, the better you can teach him, but the DISC tells us the foundational learning style. In our opinion, all the other assessments complement that one.

Chapter 23
Why Do This?

As we pointed out in the second chapter of this book, some parents become parents unintentionally. Others want children, but for unhealthy reasons, and still others have children because they want to grow a family in light of God's command to be fruitful and multiply. No matter how you came about having a child, one thing is certain: You are responsible for the growth and development of another human being. Your life is no longer the same. You have created another person who will always know you as "mom" or "dad," and until they die, they will always think of you as someone whose actions and attitudes fundamentally molded them into whoever they became.

Because this is no small responsibility, we urge parents to be purposeful in how they interact with their children. We're not suggesting you ignore your own calling; we're urging you to devote serious attention to learning as much as you can about the makeup of your student's soul while they are in your care.

What makes your child laugh? What makes your child sad? What are his strongest interests? What does he turn away from, and why? What kind of information does he notice? What kind of experiences does he seek? How does he process what he learns and what he experiences? Is he physically active, or more reserved? Is he mentally active, or more steady? How does he deal with challenges? Does he engage others easily, or is he shy?

As we've seen throughout this book, there are many, many facets of each person's makeup, and these are the subjects that we, as students of our students, must learn.

By way of reminder, no right or wrong answers exist for any of the above questions – only differences. To use the analogy of a gardener in light of Proverbs 22:6, our job as parents involves first determining what kind of plant we have, and then training up that plant in the way it grows best.

As you know, perhaps by the circumstances of your own life, too many parents never become students of their students. Consider the following story that Margie told us. Margie is in her early 50's, and as she describes it to us, she has only recently started to feel alive.

> It physically hurts inside when I think about what might have been. Growing up, I always loved writing. But when I showed my work to my parents, it was just another piece of paper to them. They'd politely nod, tell me, "That's nice," and set it aside, sometimes even in the stack of things to be thrown out. Somewhere along the way I stopped writing. It hurt when they paid no attention to what I was pouring my soul into, so why set myself up for that pain? And now that I'm in my 50's, when I look back it hurts even worse, because I realize I missed out on decades of my true calling. Essentially, I did not do much of what God designed me to do. After I got out of school I worked in retail, and never left it. Today I'm a store manager, and I make good money, so you'd think I'd be happy about that. I'm not.
>
> Thankful, yes. Happy, no.
>
> For the past three decades I've done okay, but I've always felt empty inside. It's only recently, since I started writing again, that I've started feeling what I would call "alive."
>
> When I was young, poetry was my favorite. I would think through all sorts of perspectives and write deep, meaningful verses where each line was like its own book that spoke volumes about life.

But, like I said, my parents never cared. Neither did my sister. The only people who cared were my English teachers, and at the time I thought they only showed interest because they were supposed to – because that was their job.

Today that's different. I have *finally* given myself permission to write again. I finally feel safe enough. Now I'll spend hours sitting at a picnic bench in the park, watching people, thinking, and writing. Why do I feel safer now? Maybe it's because my parents have both passed on in the last decade so I'm no longer afraid of the pain. Or, maybe God is just reminding me of the gift he once gave me that I was ignoring. Either way, I finally feel like I'm breathing fresh air. And, with whatever years I have left, I'm going to write poetry – and maybe even publish a book of it.

Margie is not alone. We talk with dozens and dozens of people who share similar stories with us. Their parents did not try to understand them, and they ended up spending decades living unfulfilled lives, doing something outside their area of natural gifting.

We ask you to consider the perspective of Margie's parents, looking down from heaven, and hearing Margie tell the above story. If you heard these words and saw the pain and regret that was in her heart, wouldn't you want to go back and show more interest in Margie's poems? Wouldn't you be selecting one of her poems as the "poem of the month," framing it, and putting it on display in your home? Wouldn't you be helping her find ways to get her work published?

To avoid the pain that resulted from not having her natural giftings acknowledged as valuable, Margie gave up much of the joy she could have had in her life.

We write this not to lay any guilt trips. We write this to shine a light on the responsibility each of us has as a parent. Our children are people. Real people. With real thoughts, real feelings, and real giftings and callings. They are not anchors or extra burdens for us to drag along as we go about our lives. We've written this book to draw your attention to the many facets that comprise your child – and yourself.

So in reality, this book is not only about becoming a student of your students. It's also a call to learn about yourself.

As we've suggested in previous chapters:

1. Identify your own tendencies and preferences
2. Identify the tendencies and preferences of your spouse
3. Identify the tendencies and preferences of your children

Becoming a student of your student requires investing your time and attention to learn what's in your children's hearts. Therefore, to make the world a better place both for you and for your children, we urge you to learn more about yourself and your spouse, and most definitely, become a student of your students, valuing them for who God made them to be.

About the Authors

Daniel and Jeralynne Bobinski are homeschooling parents living in Boise, Idaho. Since 1989, Daniel has been the owner of Leadership Development, Inc. and Workplace-Excellence.com, teaching emotional intelligence and management skills to managers and leaders in Fortune 500 companies as well as small and mid-sized companies. He writes a regular column on workplace issues, has authored several books (including the best-selling *Creating Passion-Driven Teams*), and has been interviewed by CNN Money, Fox News, and of all things, ESPN. His other line of business is workplace learning (Everything-Training.com), assisting companies in creating highly effective training programs. Daniel holds a masters degree in education from Idaho State University, and a bachelor of science degree in workforce education from Southern Illinois University. Daniel is also a certified behavioral analyst and a certified values / motivations analyst (yes, there is such a thing!).

Jeralynne holds a bachelor of science degree in psychology from Boise State University, and has been active in the homeschooling community in southern Idaho since 2007, including running a speech and debate club for homeschooled Christian teens.

In 2014, Daniel and Jeralynne founded Family Experience Ministries (FamilyExperience.net) with the stated purpose of equipping parents with tools to know, love, and lead their families. They enjoy talking to anyone who will listen about the benefits of homeschooling, how parents can build healthy relationships with their kids, and how awesome it is to have a relationship with God.

Contact Daniel & Jeralynne at familyexperience@outlook.com.

Appendix

Where to Get Assessments

In this book we mention various assessments and where to get them. So you won't have to leaf through the book every time you want to find out where to get one, we're including this reference list.

Please remember that the Internet addresses we provide here may change. That said, if you discover a link no longer works, a reliable search engine and a little bit of detective work should do the trick.

Also remember to *Know Thyself* first, as then you will know how to adapt to your learners' unique styles.

DISC Assessments – Used for measuring behavioral style, which directly correlates to learning style. Specifically, DISC measures how we respond to problems, people, pace, and procedures. Our Core style also reveals how we prefer to perceive and process information behaviorally. The assessment has 24 questions & requires approximately 10 minutes to complete.

You can obtain DISC Assessments from us at a substantial discount. Visit our website at *www.familyexperience.net* to see samples and get access to take the assessment (which are completed online). We have versions for teachers so you can know your own teaching and learning style, and student versions that provide insights into how your students learn best! *Bonus*: Our student versions include several pages of career options to consider. The program does this by comparing your student's natural behavioral style to careers enjoyed by people who have similar behavioral styles.

Hemispheric Mode Indicators – Used for identifying the hemisphere of one's brain that tends to be more dominant, and the intensity of that tendency. Knowing a student's hemisphericity enables teachers to present information in ways that are more readily absorbed by the student. The assessment has 32 questions and requires approximately 10 minutes to complete.

If you prefer paper versions, order them from *familyexperience.net*, and we will mail them to you. If you prefer online assessments, they can be found at *aboutlearning.com*. The page with a link to the assessment is *www.AboutLearning.com/assessments/hemispheric-mode-indicator*.

(*NOTE*: *aboutlearning.com* also sells paper versions, but you must buy 25 at a time.)

Multiple Intelligences – Used for identifying a relative ranking of one's interests and innate aptitudes for learning (or intellect) in nine different areas. The number of questions vary per assessment, and the time required to complete them varies from 5 – 10 minutes.

Many free assessments for this are found online, but not all are equal. We like the one found at *literacynet.org* (specifically at *http://www.literacynet.org/mi/assessment/findyourstrengths.html*).

Another useful version can be found at *BGFL.org* (specifically at *http://www.bgfl.org/bgfl/custom/resources_ftp/client_ftp/ks3/ict/multiple_int/index.htm*).

NOTE: The "Existential (Spiritual) Intelligence" was the most recent intelligence added to Gardner's list of intelligences, and most assessments do not yet test for it.

Myers-Briggs Type Indicators (MBTI) – Used for determining how a person directs energy, perceives information (cognitively), processes information (cognitively) and makes decisions. The number of questions and time required vary depending on the version of the assessment being taken.

An official MBTI must be administered by a certified practitioner. An official MBTI assessment can be found online at *www.mbtionline.com*. The cost covers both the online assessment and the accompanying interactive learning experience that explores the characteristics of your type.

For a much deeper (and more expensive) analysis, the Center for Applications of Psychological Type offers an MBTI and an hour-long phone consultation with a certified MBTI professional who will answer any questions you have. Their website is *www.capt.org*.

A close "cousin" assessment, which measures the same factors as the MBTI is the Keirsey Temperament Sorter. These assessments can be found at *www.keirsey.com*. A complementary Sorter is included in the book *Please Understand Me II* by David Keirsey. A free online version can be found at *www.passiondriventeams.com*.